# The Kids' Pocket Signing Guide

## Mickey Flodin

A PERIGEE BOOK

*To*

*my wife and son;*
*two very special people*
*in my life*

**THE BERKLEY PUBLISHING GROUP**
**Published by the Penguin Group**
**Penguin Group (USA) Inc.**
**375 Hudson Street, New York, New York 10014, USA**
Penguin Group (Canada), 90 Eglinton Avenue East, Suite 700, Toronto, Ontario M4P 2Y3, Canada
(a division of Pearson Penguin Canada Inc.)
Penguin Books Ltd., 80 Strand, London WC2R 0RL, England
Penguin Group Ireland, 25 St. Stephen's Green, Dublin 2, Ireland (a division of Penguin Books Ltd.)
Penguin Group (Australia), 250 Camberwell Road, Camberwell, Victoria 3124, Australia
(a division of Pearson Australia Group Pty. Ltd.)
Penguin Books India Pvt. Ltd., 11 Community Centre, Panchsheel Park, New Delhi—110 017, India
Penguin Group (NZ), cnr. Airborne and Rosedale Roads, Albany, Auckland 1310, New Zealand
(a division of Pearson New Zealand Ltd.)
Penguin Books (South Africa) (Pty.) Ltd., 24 Sturdee Avenue, Rosebank, Johannesburg 2196,
South Africa

Penguin Books Ltd., Registered Offices: 80 Strand, London WC2R 0RL, England

Copyright © 2004 by Mickey Flodin.
Text design and interior photos © Mickey Flodin
Cover photographs by Alexa Garbarino

PRINTING HISTORY
Perigee trade paperback edition / April 2006

ISBN: 0-399-53207-2

PERIGEE is a registered trademark of Penguin Group (USA) Inc.
The "P" design is a trademark belonging to Penguin Group (USA) Inc.

The book has been cataloged by the Library of Congress

PRINTED IN THE UNITED STATES OF AMERICA

10   9   8   7   6   5   4   3   2   1

# CONTENTS

# ACKNOWLEDGMENTS

My sincere thanks to two individuals who helped make this book possible.

Carol Flodin, my companion and best friend, who generously gave of her time to proof the final text, compile and check the index, and offer many invaluable suggestions.

John Duff, publisher, Perigee Books, for his support for this project.

## INTRODUCTION

It's a fact, kids think sign language is great and love to sign. Some kids say they feel free and alive when they sign. Others say they feel more confident because they learned to sign. Well, it's not  surprising. Signing involves, not only the brain, but the hands, arms and body get involved too. Studies show learning to sign helps kids excel in other areas also. Certainly signing is popular for we see people signing everywhere—at school, on television, in movies, in plays, in stores, and at home. Signing is fun, expressive, and rewarding to learn. But it is more, for it is a language that enables you to "talk" to people who sign but cannot hear. American Sign Language (ASL) is the native language of the Deaf community in the United States. It is a visual-gesture language that was developed over many years by deaf people to communicate with each other. It has a different syntax (word order) and the rules of grammar are different than English. ASL is preferred by deaf people when communicating among themselves.

When hearing and deaf people sign together, they usually take the signs of ASL and put them in English word order. This is easier for hearing people. This is known as Signed English (SE). SE also includes the body language and facial expressions of ASL. Although signs were originally created to represent concepts and not words, SE is an acceptable method of communication and is a good way to teach deaf children English. This signing system is combined with speech and fingerspelling.

## ABOUT THIS BOOK

*T*he *Kids' Pocket Signing Guide* has been written especially for kids to have a ready source for everyday signs to "talk with their hands" to friends, family, and anyone who is deaf. It contains the basic sign language vocabulary to express common, everyday ideas, events, and feelings. This is a book designed to be carried where ever kids go. Communication is essential, and learning to sign makes better communication possible. Wouldn't you like to know how to "talk" with your hands? Well, now you can. *The Kids' Pocket Signing Guide* will guide you step-by-step. You'll be signing in only a short time. This book will help you say, with signs, the things you say everyday. You will have fun signing across a room a secret message and showing the new signs you've learned to your friends and family.

   *The Kids' Pocket Signing Guide* contains the basic signs in use in the United States and Canada, though there may be some local variations.

   This book has eleven categorized chapters, each containing many sentences related to one or more similar subjects. The sentences were written to stand alone and do not tell a story. Many sentences contain one or two words in parentheses () and some in boxes. These words can be used in place of the previous word or phrase. Example: *Good morning (night)* can be signed *Good morning* or *Good night.* Also, the last page of each chapter (except chapters 1 and 5) has a "Try It" page for you to try combining six signs with others from the book. This gives you several possible sentences to sign. Even so, don't be afraid to be creative. If a needed sentence can't be found, combine two sentences or change a question to a statement. Also there are several games you'll have fun with.

As you begin, learn the manual alphabet first, for it will expand your ability to communicate. Also, many signs have "initialized" hand shapes such as a "C hand" (more on this later). Once you learn the manual alphabet, you can skip from chapter to chapter picking out the sentences or signs you wish or need to learn, or simply start at the beginning of the book.

Look at the illustration(s) and arrow(s) for the correct hand shape and movement of the sign. Then read the description.

Sometimes the sign is repeated, or the hands may "alternate," or they may "move together."

**The Dominant Hand**
Some signs are performed using two different hand shapes. The dominant hand provides the movement while the other hand is motionless. An example is *zoo*.

All the signs are illustrated for a right-handed person. Some left-handed people may feel it is impossible to use the right hand as the dominant hand, but making the signs with the left hand reverses the signs to the receiver. If possible, use the right hand.

**Sign Directions**
Most of the signs in this book show the sign as you would see someone signing to you. However, a number of signs are shown from an angle or profile view or close up to make the signs clearer and easier to follow. Remember to face the person you are signing with.

# SOME BASIC THINGS

**The Manual Alphabet and Fingerspelling**
One of the first things to learn in signing is the manual alphabet: it's not difficult and lots of fun (see chapter 1). I'm sure you already

*(continued on page 12)*

# THE BASIC HAND SHAPES

Throughout this book you will notice certain basic hand shapes which are used in the descriptions on how to form the signs correctly. So, it's a good idea to know these handshapes:

### *And* Hand
When the "*and* hand" is mentioned only the ending position is being referred to with all fingertips touching.

### Bent Hand
The fingers are touching and bent at the knuckles.

### Clawed Hand
The fingers are held apart and bent.

**Closed Hand**
The hand is closed
like a fist in the
shape of an *S* hand.

**Curved Hand**
The fingers are curved
and touching. Sometimes a
term such as "curved *open*
hand" is used, in which
case the fingers are kept
bent but spread apart.

**Flat Hand**
The hand is held flat
with fingers touching.

**Open Hand**
The hand is held
flat, fingers apart.
Sometimes called a
"flat *open* hand".

know some of them. Have you ever seen someone give the "victory" sign? Well, that's the letter V in sign. Many of the manual alphabet hand shapes are easy to remember because they look like the shape of English letters. Here are some others: C, I, L, M, N, O, W, Y, and Z is drawn in the air with the index finger. See, you already know several signs.

**The Signing Area**
You may be wondering where the signs are done. Well, most signs are made within an

**Signing Area**

imaginary rectangle in front of the body—an area extending from the top of the head to the waist, and just beyond the shoulders. This allows the eyes to follow the sign's movement more readily and makes the signs easier to understand. Pause when you are in between thoughts or sentences, or waiting for a response, by holding your hand in a comfortable position at chest level or at your side.

**Understanding Present, Past, and Future Time**
It is important to understand the sign language concept of present, past, and future time. Think of the area immediately

in front of the body as representing *present* time. Therefore, signs dealing with present time are made in front of the body, such as *now*. Signs referring to the future, such as *tomorrow*, have a forward movement away from the body. Signs that deal with the past, such as *last year*, move backward from the present time reference place.

### Signing Capitals
When capitals or abbreviations are finger-spelled, such as *U.S.A.*, they need to look different from other letters or words. This is done by circling (to the right) each letter slightly as you sign it.

### How to Use the *Person-Ending* Sign
The *person-ending* sign usually relates to a person's occupation, position in life, or nationality and is always used after another sign. It is made by holding both flat open hands to the front with palms facing; then move them down together. Some examples: sign *photograph* plus the *person ending* for *photographer*; sign *airplane* plus the *person ending* for *pilot*.

**Person Ending**

• • • • • • • • • • • • • • • • • • • • • • • • • • • • • • • • • • • • • • • • • • • • • • •

**Possessives and Plurals**
For the purposes of this book, possessives
('s) and plurals are generally understood
within context.

**Questions and Punctuation**
Punctuation marks, such as the period and
question mark, are not usually used in
signing. A quizzical or questioning facial
expression and body language or the
context will help convey that you are ask-
ing a question, or you can use the question
mark sign (see page 157). To indicate the
end of a thought or sentence, just pause
for a moment.

**Definite and Indefinite Articles**
Definite and indefinite articles (*a, an,* and
*the*) are often used by hearing people when
signing, especially to teach deaf students
English, but some people may prefer not to
sign them. Therefore, the signs for articles
are shown in the sentences where they
occur, but signing them is optional.

**Numbers, Money, and Years**
Money amounts, years, addresses, and
telephone numbers are signed as they are
spoken in English. To express the amount
$19.42, sign *nineteen (19) dollars four two*

• • • • • • • • • • • • • • • • • • • • • • • • • • • • • • • • • • • • • • • • • • • • • • • •

*(4-2) cents.* For the year 1996, sign *nine-teen (19) nine six (9-6).* The address 735 Lake Shore Drive is signed *7-3-5 Lake Shore Drive* (the words are signed and/or fingerspelled). The digits of a telephone number are signed as they are spoken; the number 555-3674, for example, is signed *5-5-5* (pause) *3-6-7-4.*

# TIPS FOR BETTER SIGNING

### Initialized Signs
As you begin to learn signing, you will notice that a number of signs are "initialized." The term refers to a sign formed with the fingerspelled hand shape of the first letter of the English word. Two examples are *water,* made with an W hand, and *club,* made with C hands.

**Uncle**

### The Locations of Gender Signs
The male and female gender signs are identified more easily by their locations. Many male-related signs are made near the forehead, while many female-related signs are made near the cheek or chin (see *uncle* and *aunt* at right).

**Aunt**

*(continued on page 18)*

# THE MANUAL ALPHABET

**A**      **B**      **C**      **D**      **E**

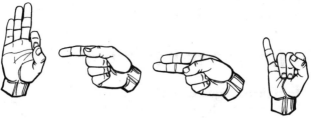

**F**      **G**      **H**      **I**

**J**      **K**      **L**      **M**

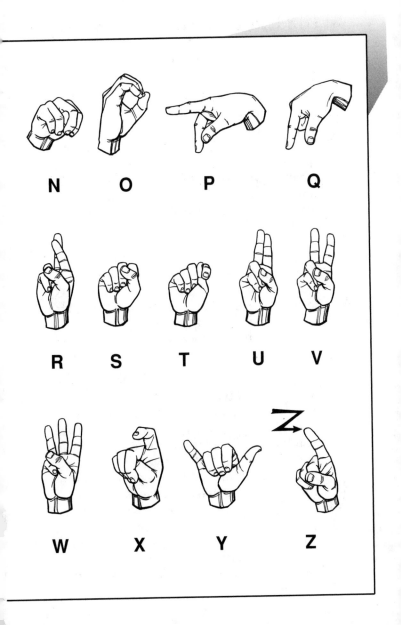

**Opposites**
You will soon discover that there are some pairs of signs that have the same hand shape, but have a reverse movement and, quite often, are opposite in meaning. Two examples are: *come* and *go*; and *open* and *close*.

**Thinking and Feeling Signs**
Signs that deal with thinking or mental activity are usually made at or near the head. An example is *imagination*. Another group of signs are those that deal with *feelings*. Many of these signs are done in the chest area near or at the heart, such as *happy*.

**You Can Do It**
Now that you know the basics, you can start signing. You will soon discover (if you haven't already) the fun, excitement, and satisfaction of "talking" with your hands. Have fun and don't worry if you forget a sign or make a few mistakes as you learn. That happens to everyone. As you sign more, you will get better and your confidence will grow. In a few short weeks, you'll even surprise yourself. I know you can do it. Have fun with *The Kids' Pocket Signing Guide*.

# Fingerspelling
# Fun &
# Name Signs 1

# FINGERSPELLING

Fingerspelling is used to spell out words one letter at a time with the manual alphabet. It is used for names of people, places, and words for which there are no signs, or as a substitute when the sign has not been learned. It is important to learn to fingerspell to communicate with deaf people. So, memorizing the manual alphabet at the beginning of learning sign language is an important first step. Since you already know some of the signs, the entire manual alphabet can be memorized in a short time. Then you can start fingerspelling two- and three-letter words before moving on to larger ones.

**Fingerspelling Position**

When fingerspelling, hold your hand in a comfortable position near the right shoulder, with the palm facing forward. Don't make exaggerated hand or arm movements. Try to combine the letters smoothly and at a comfortable rate. Pause slightly at the end of each word but do not drop the hands between words. It is important to speak or mouth the word, not the letter, as you begin to fingerspell it.

Words with double letters (*keep*) can be fingerspelled by opening the hand slightly between letters. For words with

● ● ● ● ● ● ● ● ● ● ● ● ● ● ● ● ● ● ● ● ● ● ● ● ● ● ● ● ● ● ● ● ● ● ● ● ● ● ●

double open letters, such as *will*, move the L hand to the right with a small bounce to sign the second letter *L*.

When receiving or reading fingerspelling, learn to read words in syllables rather than individual letters. This may be difficult at first but it will help you grasp the word more quickly. It is always helpful to have a friend to practice with, but when you don't, try fingerspelling in front of a mirror. This allows you to see how others see you signing.

## NAME SIGNS

Name signs are shortcuts to fingerspelling a person's name. Since fingerspelling is slower, it's good to have a name sign, especially if someone has a long name. To develop one, think of an outstanding quality you have and use your first initial. Here's an example: Trisha has long black hair. So, her name sign could be a *T* hand touching the hair or going down the right side of the head. Always fingerspell your name first, especially when meeting deaf people. Then use your name sign. Try making up one for yourself. Or you can use your full initials instead.

# Fun Stuff...

## Fingerspelling Fun

Try fingerspelling the groups of letters below. It's fun, isn't it? Now, try some larger words. If you can't think of any, use a magazine, newspaper, or dictionary.

| at | cat | dig | zip | mall | dear | will | Megan |
|----|-----|-----|-----|------|------|------|-------|
| ad | can | pig | hip | tall | hear | hill | Aaron |
| am | DVD | rig | tip | spam | near | sill | Anna |
| as | may | bay | net | x box | cake | nine | Dave |
| CD | hay | say | wet | shop | bake | mine | Tina |

## Fingerspelling Game

Here's a game you can play yourself or with a friend. Try fingerspelling store names (or street names) as you travel in the car. If your are with a friend, see who can fingerspell the most store or street names before the car stops at the next (or third) traffic light. If it's a short trip, see who can fingerspell the most before you get to your destination.

# Animals & Nature 2

The   zoo   has

tigers   and   lions.

**AND:** Move the open hand to the right as hand closes to all fingertips touching.

**HAS, HAVE, HAD:** Move the bent hands fingertips to the chest.

**LION:** Move the right curved open hand backward over the head as the hand shakes.

**THE:** Hold up the right *T* hand, palm left, and twist it to the right so palm is forward.

**TIGER:** Move the slightly curved hands apart from the center of the face ending in clawed hands at sides.

**ZOO:** Draw the letter *Z* with the right index finger on the left open palm.

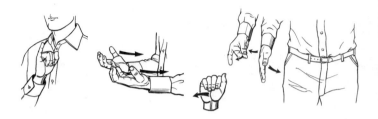

I    want    a    dog

(cat).

D   a   n

● ● ● ● ● ● ● ● ● ● ● ● ● ● ● ● ● ● ● ● ● ● ● ● ● ● ● ● ● ● ● ● ● ● ● ● ● ● ● ●

**A:** Move the right *A* hand in a small arc to the right.

**CAT:** Place the thumbs and index fingers of both *F* hands under the nose. Move them sideways.

**DAN:** Fingerspell *D-A-N*.

**DOG:** Slap right hand on right leg and snap fingers.

**I:** Place the right *I* hand on the chest, palm left.

**WANT:** Hold both curved open hands with palms up. Move both hands toward the body a few times.

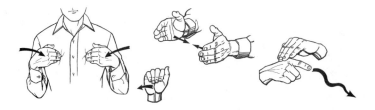

has       a       small       snake.

The  museum       has       a

• • • • • • • • • • • • • • • • • • • • • • • • • • • • • • • • • • • •

**A:** Move the right *A* hand in a small arc to the right.

**HAS, HAVE, HAD:** Move bent hands fingertips to the chest.

**MUSEUM:** Draw the shape of a house with both *M* hands, palms out.

**SMALL, LITTLE (measure, size):** Place both flat hands with palms facing. Move hands towards each other a few times.

**SNAKE:** Pass the right index finger in a weaving movement under the left palm.

**THE:** Hold up the right *T* hand, palm left, and twist it to the right so palm is forward.

big          dinosaur.          My

pet          bird          talks.

**BIG, LARGE:** Place both *L* hands in front of the chest, palms out, and draw them apart.

**BIRD:** Hold the right *Q* hand at the side of the mouth. Open and close the index finger and thumb a few times.

**DINOSAUR:** Point the left flat hand to the right with palm facing down. Rest the right elbow on the back of the left hand with the right arm held up. Move right bent *and* hand back and forth a few times.

**MY, MINE, OWN:** Place the right flat hand on the chest.

**PET:** Stroke the back of the left hand with the fingers of the right hand once or twice.

**TALK:** Move both index fingers alternately back and forth from the mouth, palms facing in.

My      favorite      animal

is   a   <u>horse.</u>   kangaroo

*Use any of the following signs.*

**A:** *(See page 26.)*

**ANIMAL:** With fingertips on the chest, rock both bent hands in and out sideways.

**FAVORITE:** Touch chin several times with right middle finger.

**HORSE:** Place the thumb of right *U* hand on right temple and bend the *U* fingers up and down several times.

**IS:** Place right *I* hand at the mouth and move it forward.

**KANGAROO:** Move the right bent hand forward in a double arc movement. Two hands can be used.

**MY, MINE, OWN:** Place the right flat hand on the chest.

deer

monkey

bear

fox

**BEAR:** Form clawed hands and cross the arms at the chest. Then make clawing movements toward the center of the chest.

**DEER, ANTLERS:** Touch the thumbs of the open hands at the temples a couple times with palms forward.

**FOX, SLY:** Place the *F* hand over the nose and twist toward the left.

**MONKEY, APE:** Form claw-shaped hands and scratch the sides of the body.

  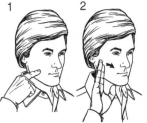

Spiders　(bugs)　scare

me.　Look;　<u>bee</u>

*Use any of the following signs.*

**BEE:** Place the right index finger on right cheek, then brush right flat-hand fingers forward across the cheek.

**BUG, INSECT:** Place the thumb of the right *3* hand on the nose. Move the index finger and middle fingers up and down several times.

**ME:** Point to or touch the chest with right index finger.

**SCARE, SCARED, AFRAID:** Place the *and* hands at the sides of the chest, palms facing. Move them together as they change to open hands with palms facing the body.

**SPIDER:** Cross curved open hands, palms down, and interlock little fingers. Then wiggle the fingers. Hands can move forward also.

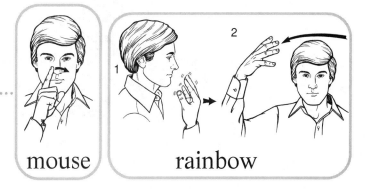

mouse

rainbow

falling

star.

**FALL (verb):** Place the right *V* fingers upright on flat left palm. Turn over *V* hand laying its back on flat left palm.

**LOOK, LOOK AT, LOOK AT ME, LOOK BACK, LOOK DOWN, WATCH:** Point the *V* hand to the eyes. Twist the *V* hand and point it forward. For *look at me*, *look back*, and *look down*, point the *V* hand at the eyes, then in the direction needed.

**RAINBOW:** Wiggle the fingers of the right open hand in front of the mouth as the hand moves forward. Place the right open hand over the head and move it to right.

**STAR:** Alternately strike sides of both index fingers as they move upward in front of face.

**MOUSE:** Move the right index finger across the nose several times.

  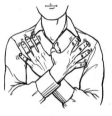

We    built    a    tree

 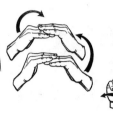

house.    Beautiful    butterfly

**A:** Move the right *A* hand in a small arc to the right.

**BEAUTIFUL, HANDSOME, PRETTY:** Place the right *and* hand fingertips at chin. Open hand as it circles face ending with *and* hand. The *H* hand can be used for *handsome*.

**BUILT, BUILD:** Place bent hand fingers, palms down on top of each other a few times as they move up a little.

**BUTTERFLY:** Cross both open hands in front of chest and interlock thumbs. Wiggle fingers .

**HOUSE:** Outline the shape of a house with the flat hands.

**TREE:** Hold the right hand upright with left hand under the right elbow and wiggle the fingers of the right hand.

**WE, US:** *(See page 34.)*

(flower). The    sun    is

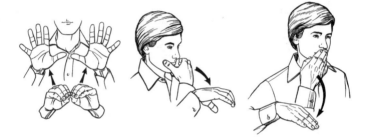

bright.    Hot    (bad)

- - - - - - - - - - - - - - - - - - - - - - - - - - - - - - - - - - - - - -

**BAD:** Touch lips with finger-tips of right flat hand. Then turn hand and move it down with the palm facing down.

**BRIGHT, LIGHT:** Place *and* hands in front. Move them up and apart to open hands.

**FLOWER:** Move fingertips of right *and* hand from under one nostril then the other.

**HOT, HEAT:** Hold the right *C* hand at the mouth and quick-ly turn it forward to the right.

**IS:** Place right *I* hand at the mouth and move it forward.

**SUN:** Make a left to right cir-cle above the head with right index finger pointing forward.

**THE:** *(See page 26.)*

weather.   It   is

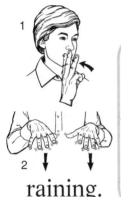

raining.   lightning   snowing

*Use any sign at right.*

**IS:** *(See page 35.)*

**IT:** Touch the right *I* finger in the flat left palm.

**LIGHTNING:** Quickly draw a jagged line in the air with the right index finger.

**RAIN:** Sign *water* by touching right side of mouth a couple of times with right *W* index finger. Wiggle fingers of both hands as they move down. Some signers don't sign

*water* first.

**SNOW:** Place curved open hand on chest. Move it forward to an *and* hand. Move open hands down as fingers wiggle.

**WE, US:** Circle right *W* hand from the right side of chest, palm left, in an arc to the left side of the chest with fingers pointing up. End with palm facing right. Use *U* hand for *us*.

**WEATHER:** *(See page 35.)*

# Summer is here.

*Use any sign below.*

winter | fall | spring

**FALL, AUTUMN:** Slide the right flat hand index finger down the left forearm which is held in front at an angle.

**HERE:** Move both flat hands, palms up, in opposite forward circles in front of the body.

**IS:** Place the right *I* hand at the mouth and move it forward.

**SPRING, GROW:** Pass the right *and* hand up and through the left *C* hand while opening the fingers of the right hand.

**SUMMER:** Wipe the curved right index finger, from left to right, across the forehead.

**WEATHER:** Face both *W* hands and twist them up and down.

**WINTER, COLD:** Shake both *S* hands in front of the chest.

# *Fun Stuff...*

## Which Animal Is It?

All the signs are animals. Can you name them?
Read hints and directions below, then write the
name below each sign. The first letter is given and
a few are pictured. Answers on page 191.

**1.** E _____

**2.** R _____

**3.** B _____

**4.** F _____

**5.** G _____

**1.** (Hint: big) Hold back of the
right curved hand at mouth,
palm down. Move it forward a
little then down and up.

**2.** (Hint: long ears) Cross both
*H* hands at the wrists, palms
in. Bend the *H* fingers together a couple times.

**3.** (Hint: flight) Hold right *Q*
hand at side of mouth. Open
and close index finger and
thumb a few times.

**4.** (Hint: good jumper) Hold
right *S* hand under the chin,
palm in. Flip out the index
and middle fingers together.

**5.** (Hint: long) Put left *C* hand
on neck. Place right *C* hand
on top of the left.
Move right hand
forward and
upward. You can
use right hand only.

6

O

7

T

9

E

8

D

11

F

10

P

forward. Open and close
the *N* fingers and thumb a
couple times.

**6.** (Hint: large eyes) Hold *O*
hands up and look through
them. Twist hands back and
forth several times.

**7.** (Hint: always home) Place
curved left hand on the right
*A* hand, and wiggle the right
thumb up and down.

**8.** (Hint: walks funny) Place
right *N* fingers and thumb in
front of mouth: fingers point

**9.** (Hint: nation's symbol)
With palm forward, hold right
*X* hand in front of nose.

**10.** (Hint: mud) Bend and
unbend the flat hand under
the chin a few times.

**11.** (Hint: water) Hold the left
flat hand fingers at the wrist
(or elbow) of the right flat
hand. Both hands point forward. Move the right hand
back and forth from the wrist.

# Try It

Make up sentences using these signs with others in the book.

moon    sky    environment

ocean    earth    mountain

**EARTH:** Hold the left closed hand between right index finger and thumb and rock the right hand from left to right.

**ENVIRONMENT:** Move right *E* hand in a circle around left vertical index finger.

**MOON:** Place the right *C* hand around the right eye.

**MOUNTAIN, HILL:** Hit the back of the closed left hand with the closed right hand.

Next, make upward wavy movements with both open hands in front of the body.

**OCEAN:** Place index finger of the right *W* hand on the right side of the mouth several times. Then make forward wavy movements with both curved hands, palms down.

**SKY, HEAVENS, SPACE:** Move right flat hand above head in an arc, left to right.

# Sports, Hobbies 3
# & Recreation

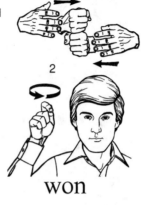

We          won          the

baseball          game.          basketball

*Use any of the following signs.*

**BASEBALL, BAT, SOFTBALL:** Make two *S* hands. Place right hand on left and swing forward as if hitting a ball.

**BASKETBALL:** Move both curved open hands upward and forward.

**GAME, CHALLENGE:** Bring the knuckles of both *A* hands together from sides of chest.

**THE:** Twist right *T* hand from palm left to palm forward.

**WE, US:** Circle the right *W* hand from the right side of the chest, palm left, in an arc to the left side of the chest with fingers pointing up. End with palm facing right. Use the *U* hand for *us*.

**WON, WIN:** Bring open hands together forming *S* hands, one over the other. Then make small circles with the raised index fingertip and thumb tip touching.

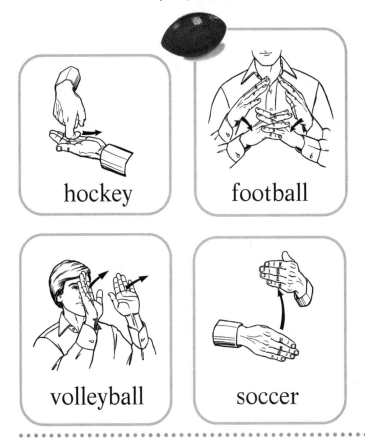

hockey

football

volleyball

soccer

**FOOTBALL:** Interlock the open hands in front of the chest a few times, palms down.

**HOCKEY:** Swing the right *X* finger across the left flat palm several times.

**SOCCER, KICK:** Strike the little finger of the left flat hand with the index side of the right flat hand with an upward swing.

**VOLLEYBALL:** Move both flat hands forward and upward in front of the face.

Play          ball.          Throw.

Catch.          I          collect

**BALL, ROUND:** Touch the fingertips of both curved open hands in the shape of a ball.

**CATCH, CAPTURE, GRAB:** The curved open hand moves quickly into an *S* hand as it rests on the back of the closed left hand.

**COLLECT, EARN:** Move the right curved hand across the left flat hand. The right hand can end in a closed position.

**I:** Place right *I* hand on chest.

**PLAY, RECREATION:** Hold up the *Y* hands. Shake them back and forth at the wrists.

**THROW:** Form an *S* hand near the right side and throw the hand forward while changing it to an open hand.

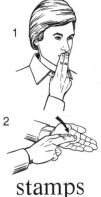

stamps        (coins).        I

like          art          class.

● ● ● ● ● ● ● ● ● ● ● ● ● ● ● ● ● ● ● ● ● ● ● ● ● ● ● ● ● ● ● ● ● ● ● ● ●

**ART, ARTIST, DRAW:** Draw a wavy line with right *I* finger over left flat palm. For *artist*, use the *person ending* after signing *art*.

**CLASS, GROUP:** Place *C* hands, palms facing; move them in a forward circle until the hands touch. *Group* can be made with *G* hands.

**COINS:** Draw a small circle with the right index finger in the left flat palm.

**I:** *(See page 42 at left.)*

**LIKE, ADMIRE:** Hold the thumb and index finger of the right open hand on the chest. Move hand forward, closing the thumb and index finger.

**STAMPS (postal):** Touch right *U* fingers to lips and then on the palm of the left flat hand.

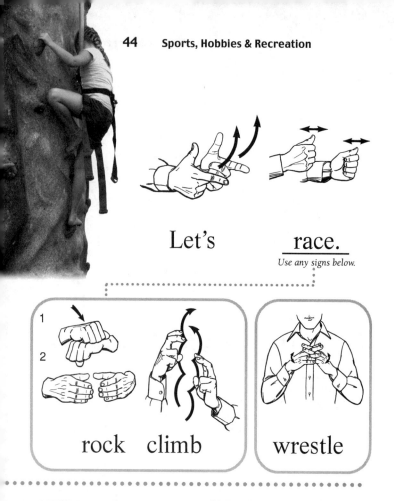

Let's     <u>race.</u>

*Use any signs below.*

rock climb       wrestle

**LET'S, LET US:** Face both *L* hands to the front with palms facing each other and several inches apart. Move them together so fingers point slightly up.

**RACE, COMPETITION, CONTEST:** Move both *A* hands back and forth alternately in front of the body, palms facing.

**ROCK CLIMB:** Sign *Rock* by hitting the back of the closed left hand with the closed right hand. Face both *C* hands slightly apart. Sign *Climb* by facing both curved *V* hands and make a climbing motion, one hand over the other.

**WRESTLE, WRESTLER:** With hands in front of chest and fingers interlocked, move hands back and forth. Add *person ending* for *wrestler*.

Run      fast.      Start.

Everyone            hide.

**EVERYONE, EVERYBODY:**
Rub the right *A* hand knuckles down the left *A* hand thumb a few times. Then point the right index finger up.

**FAST, QUICK:** Flip the right thumb from the bent index finger.

**HIDE:** Place the *A* hand thumb on the lips and move it forward under the left, palm down, curved hand.

**RUN:** Place both flat hands together palm to palm with left hand on top. Then quickly move the right hand forward.

**START, BEGIN:** Twist the right *one* hand index finger in the *V* shape of the flat left hand.

# We    went    fishing.

*Use any of the following signs.*

## skiing

## roller skating

**FISHING:** Place left modified *A* hand on right modified *A* hand and pretend to be fishing by moving hands back and forward, or flick up hands.

**ROLLER SKATING:** Move the curved *V* hands, with palms up, back and forth alternately in front of the body.

**SKIING:** Place both *S* hands at the sides and a little to the front with arms bent. Push both hands down and backward together.

**WE, US:** Circle the right *W* hand from the right side of the chest, palm left, in an arc to the left side of the chest with fingers pointing up. End with palm facing right. Use the *U* hand for *us*.

**WENT, GO:** Circle the index fingers around each other as they move forward.

boating

skateboarding

ice skating

horseback
riding

- - - - - - - - - - - - - - - - - - - - - - - - - - - - - - - - - - - - - - - - - - - - - - - - - -

**BOATING, BOAT:** Move both cupped hands forward in a bouncing motion.

**HORSEBACK RIDING:** Straddle the *V* fingers over the left *B* hand in front of the body. Move both hands forward in small arcs.

**ICE SKATING:** Move both *X* hands back and forth alternately in front of the body, palms facing up.

**SKATEBOARDING, SKATE-BOARD:** Place right *H* fingers on top of left *H* fingers and move hands ahead together in a wavy motion.

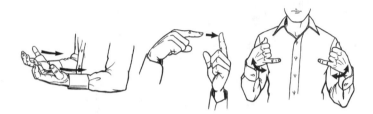

# Want          to          play

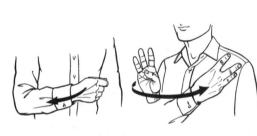

# ping-pong?   We          are

• • • • • • • • • • • • • • • • • • • • • • • • • • • • • • • • • • • • • • • • • • •

**ARE:** Move the *R* hand forward from the lips.

**PING-PONG, TABLE TENNIS:** Move the modified *A* hand back and forth as if playing ping-pong.

**PLAY, RECREATION:** Hold up the *Y* hands. Shake them back and forth at the wrists.

**TO:** Touch the left vertical index fingertip with the right index fingertip.

**WANT:** Hold both curved open hands with palms up. Move both hands toward the body a few times.

**WE, US:** Circle the right *W* hand from the right side of the chest, palm left, in an arc to the left side of the chest with fingers pointing up. End with palm facing right. Use the *U* hand for *us*.

playing cards. What music

do you like?

**DO, DID, DONE:** Move both C hands, palms down, in unison to the left then to right.

**LIKE, ADMIRE:** Hold the thumb and index finger of right open hand on the chest. Move hand forward, closing the thumb and index finger.

**MUSIC, SING, SONG:** Swing the right flat hand back and forth in front of left flat hand.

**PLAYING CARDS:** Pretend to deal cards. Hold both modified A hands (thumbs in the bend of index fingers) with right hand in front of left. Move right hand forward a few times ending with a palm up 3 hand.

**WHAT:** Move the tip of the right index finger down across the left flat palm.

**YOU:** Point to the person you are signing to.

J e n     takes     piano

(guitar)     lessons.     Drums

**DRUMS:** Hold both modified *A* hands (thumbs in bends of index fingers) to the front. Move them alternately up and down as if playing drums.

**GUITAR:** Pretend to be strumming a guitar by holding the left hand up, fingers curled and moving the right *A* hand up and down.

**JEN:** Fingerspell *J-E-N*.

**LESSON:** Rest the edge of the right flat hand across the fingers of the left flat hand and move it in a small arc to the base of the left palm.

**PIANO:** Place the curved open hands to the front and move them right and left while striking the hands down at imaginary piano keys.

**TAKE:** Move the open hand from right to left ending with a closed hand near the body.

are          fun.          We

rode          bikes          all day.

•  •  •  •  •  •  •  •  •  •  •  •  •  •  •  •  •  •  •  •  •  •  •  •  •  •  •  •  •

**ALL DAY, DAY:** Hold the left arm flat, index finger pointing right. Place the elbow of the bent right arm on left index finger. Start with the index finger far to the right and move right arm across the body in a full arc resting on the left arm.

**ARE:** Move the *R* hand forward from the lips.

**BIKE, BICYCLE:** Make two *S* hands in front of the chest with the palms down. Then move them in forward alternating circles like pedaling.

**FUN:** Brush nose with right *U* fingers. Then brush the left and right *U* fingers against each other several times.

**RIDE (a bicycle):** Hold left flat hand pointing forward and straddle the right *V* hand over it. Move hands forward a little.

**WE, US:** *(See page 48.)*

The  movie    was        good

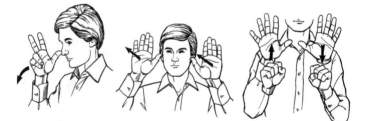

(lousy).   Awesome  fireworks.

**AWESOME, EXCELLENT, FANTASTIC:** Push both flat open hands forward and up several times, palms out.

**FIREWORKS:** Hold the *S* hands with palms facing forward. Open and close each hand as they move up and down one after another.

**GOOD:** Touch the lips with the right flat hand. Bring the right hand down into the left hand, palms up.

**LOUSY, ROTTEN:** Place the *3* hand thumb on the nose and quickly move it downward in an arc.

**MOVIE:** Face the palm of the left open hand almost forward. Place the right open hand on the left hand and move the right hand back and forth.

**WAS:** *(See page 53 at right.)*

| Can | you | go |
| --- | --- | --- |

| swimming? | Maybe. | Can't. |
| --- | --- | --- |

**CAN, COULD:** Move both *S* (or *A*) hands down together.

**CANNOT, IMPOSSIBLE:** Move the right index finger down, hitting the left index finger as it continues past the left finger.

**GO, WENT:** Circle the index fingers around each other as they move forward.

**MAYBE, MAY, POSSIBLY:** Move the flat hands up and down alternately.

**WAS:** Move the *W* hand backward near the right cheek and close it to an *S* hand.

**SWIMMING:** Point the hands forward and make the motion of swimming.

**YOU:** Point to the person you are signing to. Move the hand left to right for more than one person.

# Fun Stuff...

## Match 'em Up

Several thoughts are signed. Can you match up the sentences with the correct signs? Answers on page 191.

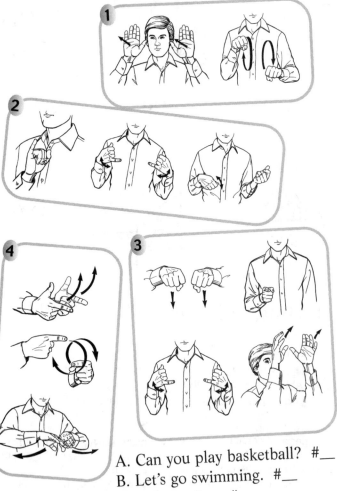

A. Can you play basketball?  #___

B. Let's go swimming.  #___

C. I play guitar.  #___

D. Awesome bike.  #___

# My Family & Friends 4

# Hi.          I          am

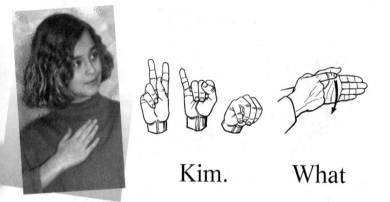

# Kim.          What

**AM:** Move the right *A* hand thumb forward from the lips.

**HI, HELLO:** Place the right *B* hand at the forehead and move it to the right. Or fingerspell *H–I*.

**I:** Place the right *I* hand on the chest, palm left.

**KIM:** Fingerspell *K-I-M*.

**WHAT:** Move the tip of the right index finger down across the left flat palm.

**YOUR, YOURS, HIS, HER, THEIR:** Push the right flat palm forward toward the person being spoken to. If it is not clear from the context, the *male* or *female* sign can be used first. When using *your* in the plural, push the right flat palm forward, then move it to the right.

is         your        name      (phone

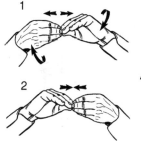

number)?      Where        do

**DO, DID, DONE:** Move both *C* hands together, palms down, to the left then to the right.

**IS:** Place right *I* hand at the mouth and move it forward.

**NAME:** Cross both *H* fingers.

**NUMBER, DIGIT:** Touch the fingertips of both flat *O* hands in front of the chest, the right palm angled in and the left palm angled forward.

Pull the hands apart a little while twisting the hands in opposite directions touching the fingertips again.

**PHONE, TELEPHONE, CALL:** Hold the thumb of the right *Y* hand to the ear.

**WHERE:** Point the right index finger up and shake it quickly back and forth.

**YOUR:** *(See page 56 at left.)*

you          live?          How

old          are          you?

**ARE:** Move the *R* hand forward from the lips.

**HOW:** Place both bent hands together back to back. Turn them forward until the hands are flat, palms up.

**LIVE, ADDRESS:** Move the *L* hands up the chest together. Use *A* hands for *address*.

**OLD, AGE:** Pretend to be grabbing a beard. Then move the right hand down from

under the chin ending with an *S* hand.

**WHEN:** Move the right index finger around the left upright index finger. Then touch the tip of the right index finger on the tip of the left index finger.

**YOU:** Point to the person you are signing to. Move the hand left to right for more than one person.

Guess.    I    am    12.

When    is    your

- - - - - - - - - - - - - - - - - - - - - - - - - - - - - -

**AM:** Move the right *A* hand thumb forward from the lips.

**GUESS:** Move the *C* hand across the front of the forehead, ending with an *S* hand.

**I:** Place the right *I* hand on the chest, palm left.

**IS:** Place right *I* hand at the mouth and move it forward.

**TWELVE:** Hold up the right *S* hand, palm facing self. Flick

index and middle fingers up.

**WHEN:** *(See page 58.)*

**YOUR, YOURS, HIS, HER, THEIR:** Push the right flat palm forward toward person being spoken to. If it is not clear from the context, the *male* or *female* sign can be used first. When using *your* in the plural, push right flat palm forward, then to right.

birthday?          Can

you          sign?          Good

**BIRTHDAY:** With palms up, hold the right hand in the left hand and move them forward and up. Bend the left arm pointing the index finger right. Bend and rest the right elbow on the left index finger with the right index finger pointing up. Move right arm in a short arc across chest.

**CAN, ABLE, COULD:** Move both *S* (or *A*) hands down together.

**GOOD:** Touch lips with right flat hand. Bring right hand down into left hand, palms up.

**SIGN (language):** Point the index fingers toward each other, palms out. Rotate them in alternating backward circles.

**YOU:** Point to person you are signing to. Move the hand left to right for more than one person.

morning    (night).    Come

to        my        party

**COME:** Circle index fingers as they move toward the body.

**MORNING:** Rest the left hand in the bend of the right arm. Hold right hand flat and arm bent horizontally. Move right arm upright, palm facing self.

**MY, MINE, OWN:** Place the right flat hand on the chest.

**NIGHT, EVENING:** Place the right curved hand over the flat horizontal left hand.

**PARTY:** Swing *P* hands left and right with palms down.

**TO:** Touch right index fingertip to left vertical index fingertip.

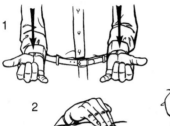

tonight.     Yes.     No.

Please.     Ask     Dad

**ASK, REQUEST:** Place the flat hands together and move them toward you.

**DAD, FATHER:** Touch the thumb of the right open hand on the forehead.

**NO:** Touch the right middle and index fingers with the thumb.

**PLEASE:** Put the right hand over the heart and move it in a small circle.

**TONIGHT:** Sign *this* and *night*. With palms up, move both *Y* (or flat) hands down at the same time. Place the right curved hand over the left horizontal flat hand and point down.

**YES:** Move the right *S* hand up and down.

(Mom).        Goodbye.        We

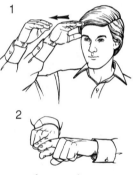

are        brothers        (twins).

**ARE:** Move the *R* hand forward from the lips.

**BROTHER:** Place the right flattened *C* hand at the forehead and close fingers. Hand can move forward a little. Next place the index fingers together.

**GOODBYE:** Bend the right flat hand up and down.

**MOM, MOTHER:** Touch the thumb of the right open hand against the chin.

**TWINS:** Place the *T* hand at the left side, then the right side of the chin.

**WE, US:** Circle the right *W* hand from the right side of the chest, palm left, in an arc to the left side of the chest with fingers pointing up. End with palm facing right. Use the *U* hand for *us*.

That     <u>girl</u>     (boy)

*Use any boxed sign.*

(baby)     is     cute.

**BABY, INFANT:** Pretend to be holding and rocking a baby with right arm on left.

**BOY, MALE:** Place the right flattened *C* hand at the forehead and close fingers. Hand can move forward a little.

**CUTE:** Move the *U* fingertips over the chin a few times.

**GIRL, FEMALE:** Slide the right *A* hand thumb along the right side of the jaw to the chin.

**IS:** Place right *I* hand at the mouth and move it forward.

**THAT:** Place the right *Y* hand in the left flat palm.

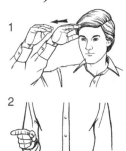
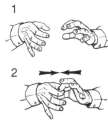
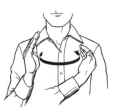

Join     our     club.

He     is     deaf

**CLUB, CLASS, GROUP:** Place *C* hands in front of chest, palms facing. Move them in a forward circle until hands touch.

**DEAF:** Point to or touch right ear. Place both flat hands slightly apart, palms forward, and bring together.

**HE, HIM:** Pretend to be gripping a cap with right hand. Move it forward a little. Point right index forward. If gender is obvious, omit gripping cap.

**IS:** Place the right *I* hand at mouth and move it forward.

**JOIN, UNITE:** Connect the thumbs and index fingers of both hands like a chain link. Keep other fingers extended.

**OUR:** Move the slightly cupped right hand in a semi-circle from the right side to the left side of the chest.

(hearing).  We  are

 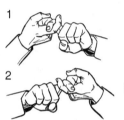 

best  friends.  That

- - - - - - - - - - - - - - - - - - - - - - - - - - - - - - - - - - - - -

**ARE:** Move the *R* hand forward from the lips.

**BEST:** Place right flat hand fingertips on the mouth. Slide it off to an *A* hand slightly above the right side of head.

**FRIEND, FRIENDSHIP:** Hook the right index finger over the left index finger, then reverse the movement.

**HEARING (person):** Move the right index finger in a forward circle from the mouth.

**THAT:** Place the right *Y* hand in the left flat palm.

**WE, US:** Circle the right *W* hand from the right side of the chest, palm left, in an arc to the left side of the chest with fingers pointing up. End with palm facing right. Use the *U* hand for *us*.

is          a          cool       haircut.

My              aunt              and

• • • • • • • • • • • • • • • • • • • • • • • • • • • • • • • • •

**A:** Move the right *A* hand in a small arc to the right.

**AND:** Move the open hand to the right as hand closes to all fingertips touching.

**AUNT:** Shake the right *A* hand near the right cheek.

**COOL:** Hold the thumb of the right open flat hand on the chest, palm left, and wiggle the fingers.

**HAIRCUT:** Place the right *H* fingers near the hair and open and close them a few times.

**IS:** Place the right *I* hand at the mouth and move it forward.

**MY, MINE, OWN:** Place the right flat hand on the chest.

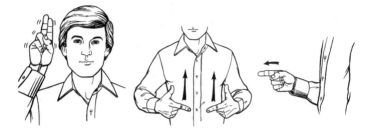

uncle          live          there.

I love you.          I          feel

**FEEL, FEELING:** Move the right middle finger of the open hand up the chest.

**I:** Place the right *I* hand on the chest, palm left.

**I LOVE YOU:** Hold up right hand with thumb, index finger, and little finger extended.

**LIVE, ADDRESS:** Move the *L* hands up the chest together.

**THERE:** Point with the right index finger to an imaginary object.

**UNCLE:** Shake right *U* hand, palm forward, near right temple.

sick.

*Use any of the boxed signs.*

dizzy

awful

My         throat         is

**AWFUL, TERRIBLE, TRAGIC:** Hold the *O* hands at the temples and fling the fingers forward to open hands, palms facing.

**DIZZY:** Move the right curved open hand in a few circles in front of the face, palm towards face.

**IS:** Place the right *I* hand at mouth and move it forward.

**MY, MINE, OWN:** Place the right flat hand on the chest.

**SICK, DISEASE, ILL:** Touch the forehead with the right middle finger and the stomach with the left middle finger.

**THROAT:** Place the right extended *G* hand fingers on the top of the throat, palm in, and move hand down the length of the throat.

sore.

It

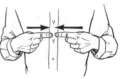
hurts.

My

feet

(hands)

**FEET:** Point to each foot.

**HANDS:** Slide the right flat hand toward self over the back of the left hand. Reverse hands and repeat the same movement.

**HURT, ACHE, INJURY, PAIN:** Jab the index fingers at each other a few times in front of body or near pain.

**IT:** Touch the right *I* finger in the flat left palm.

**MY, MINE, OWN:** Place the right flat hand on the chest.

**SORE:** Put the tip of the *A* hand thumb on the chin and twist it from side to side.

were     cold.     The

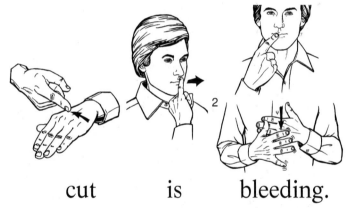

cut     is     bleeding.

**BLEED, BLOOD:** Touch the lips with the right index finger. Then, move the wiggling fingers of the right open hand over the back of the left open hand.

**COLD, CHILLY, WINTER:** Shake the upheld *S* hands in front of the chest.

**CUT:** Move the right index fingertip, palm left, across the back of the left flat hand or any place where there is a cut.

**IS:** Place the right *I* hand at the mouth and move it forward.

**THE:** Twist right *T* hand from palm left to palm forward.

**WERE:** Hold the right *W* to the front, palm left. Move it backward as it changes to an *R* hand.

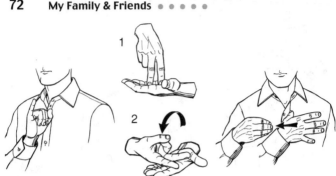

I      fell      and

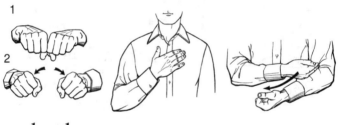

broke      my      arm.

**AND:** Move the open hand to the right as hand closes to all fingertips touching.

**ARM:** Move the fingertips of the right curved back hand down the left arm.

**BREAK, FRACTURE:** Place the *S* hands to the front and touching. Twist them quickly down and apart like *breaking* a branch.

**FALL (verb):** Place the right *V* fingers upright on the flat left palm. Turn over the *V* hand laying its back on the flat left palm.

**I:** Place the right *I* hand on the chest, palm left.

**MY, MINE, OWN:** Place the right flat hand on the chest.

# Fun Stuff...
## Find The Names

Hidden in the grid are at least 21 fingerspelled names. How many can you find? Each sign is used at least once. The names go up, down, diagonal, across, and back. Circle each one and check answers on page 191.

# Try It

Make up sentences using these signs
with others in the book.

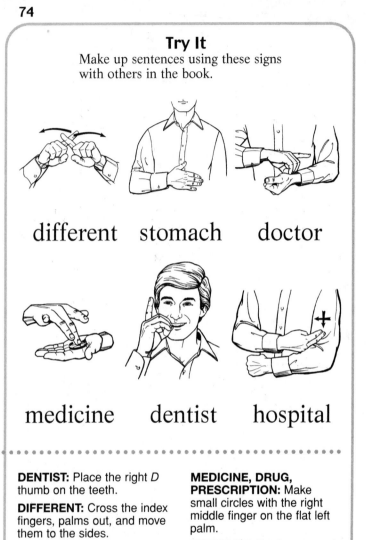

different    stomach    doctor

medicine    dentist    hospital

**DENTIST:** Place the right *D*
thumb on the teeth.

**DIFFERENT:** Cross the index
fingers, palms out, and move
them to the sides.

**DOCTOR:** Hold the *D* or *M*
fingertips on the left pulse.

**HOSPITAL:** Draw a cross on
the upper left arm with the
right *H* hand.

**MEDICINE, DRUG,
PRESCRIPTION:** Make
small circles with the right
middle finger on the flat left
palm.

**STOMACH:** Pat the stomach
with the right flat hand.

# Religion 5

What        church    (temple)

do          you          go

• • • • • • • • • • • • • • • • • • • • • • • • • • • • • • • • • • • • •

**CHURCH, CHAPEL:** Touch the right *C* hand thumb on the back of the left *S* hand.

**DO, DID, DONE:** Move both *C* hands, palms down, in unison to the left then to the right.

**GO:** Circle the index fingers around each other as they move forward.

**TEMPLE (building):** Hold the base of the right *T* hand on the back of palm down left closed hand.

**WHAT:** Move the tip of the right index finger down across the left flat palm.

**YOU:** Point to the person you are signing to. Move the hand left to right for more than one person.

to?        I        believe

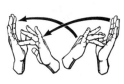

in        God        (Jesus).

**BELIEVE:** Touch the forehead with the right index finger; then place both hands together, right on left, in front of the chest.

**GOD:** Point the right *G* hand upward (or flat hand). Move it down to the chest ending in a *B* hand.

**I:** Place the right *I* hand on the chest, palm left.

**IN:** Place the right *and* hand fingertips into the left *C* hand.

**JESUS:** Place both hands to the front with palms facing. Touch the right middle finger to the left palm; then touch the left middle finger to the right palm.

**TO:** Touch the left vertical index fingertip with the right index fingertip.

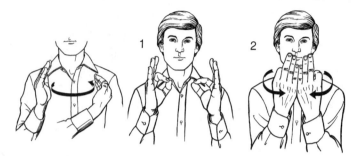

Our              family

prays    together.    I

**FAMILY:** Hold both *F* hands facing each other. Then circle both hands forward until little fingers touch.

**I:** Place the right *I* hand on the chest, palm left.

**IS:** Place the right *I* hand at the mouth and move it forward.

**OUR:** Move the slightly cupped right hand in a semi-circle from the right side to the left side of the chest.

**PRAY:** Place both flat hands together; then bow and move the hands towards self at the same time.

**TOGETHER:** Hold *A* hands together, palms facing, and circle them from right to left.

**WAS:** Move the *W* hand backward near the right cheek and close it to an *S* hand.

was     baptized.     Kids

celebrate Christmas (Hanukkah).

**BAPTIZE,:** Hold the closed *S* (or *and*) hand above the head. Quickly move it down ending with the open hand.

**CELEBRATE:** Hold up the right hand with thumb and index finger touching. Move the hand in small circles.

**CHRISTMAS:** Move the right *C* hand from left to right in a small arc.

**HANUKKAH:** Point both *H* hands down with palms down, and swing them up to 4 hands, palms in.

**KID:** Hold the right hand with index and little fingers extended, palm down. Place the index finger under the nose and move the hand up and down slightly.

**WAS:** *(See page 78 at left.)*

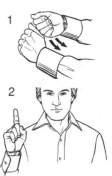

Bring    your    Bible.

God    loves    everyone.

• • • • • • • • • • • • • • • • • • • • • • • • • • • • • • • • • • •

**BIBLE:** With palms facing, touch the left palm with the right middle finger; then touch right palm with the left middle finger. Close both flat hands palm to palm, then open them.

**BRING:** Move both open hands either toward self, another person, or in direction needed, palms up, with one hand a little ahead of the other.

**EVERYONE, EVERYBODY:** Rub right *A* hand knuckles down left *A* hand thumb a few times. Then sign number one.

**GOD:** Point the right *G* hand upward. Move it down to the chest ending in a *B* hand.

**LOVES, LOVE:** Cross *S* hands at the wrists over the heart.

**YOUR, YOURS, HIS, HER, THEIR:** Push the right flat palm forward toward the person being spoken to.

# Home Things 6

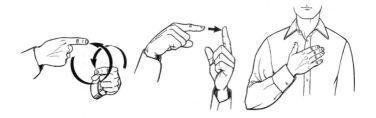

Come          to          my

house.        I          have

**COME:** Circle the index fingers as they move toward the body.

**HAVE, HAD, HAS:** Move the bent hands fingertips to the chest.

**HOUSE:** Outline the shape of a house with the flat hands.

**I:** Place the right *I* hand on the chest, palm left.

**MY, MINE, OWN:** Place the right flat hand on the chest.

**TO:** Touch the left vertical index fingertip with the right index fingertip.

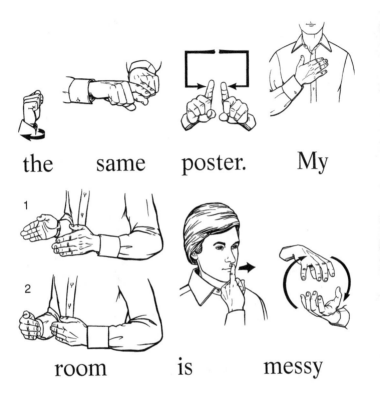

the     same     poster.     My

room     is     messy

**IS:** Place right *I* hand at the mouth and move it forward.

**MESSY, MESS UP:** Place the right curved open hand, palm down, over the left curved open hand, then switch left over right.

**MY, MINE, OWN:** Place the right flat hand on the chest.

**POSTER, SIGN:** Place both index fingers side by side and pointing up with palms forward and draw a square.

**SAME, ALIKE:** Place both index fingers together, palms down.

**ROOM:** With palms facing, hold the flat hands to the front. Then move the hands, placing the left behind the right and parallel. The *R* hands can be used.

**THE:** Twist right *T* hand from palm left to palm forward.

  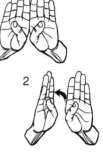

(clean).   Close   door.

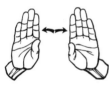  

Open   window.   See

**CLEAN, NICE:** Pass the flat right hand, palm down, over the flat left hand, palm up, from wrist to fingertips.

**CLOSE, SHUT:** Place both flat hands with palms forward, slightly apart and bring them together.

**DOOR:** Place the B hands to the front, palms out, and side-by-side. Turn the right hand back and forth.

**OPEN:** Hold both flat hands with palms forward and index finger and thumbs touching. Move hands apart.

**SEE, SIGHT, VISION:** Point the right V fingertips toward the eyes. Then move the hand forward.

**WINDOW:** Place the right flat hand on the left flat hand and move the right up a little, palms face in.

my          new          bracelet.

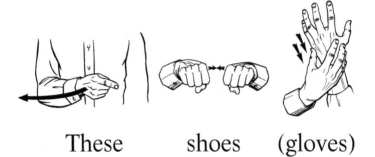

These          shoes          (gloves)

**BRACELET:** Wrap the curved index finger and thumb of the right open hand around the left wrist. Rotate right hand forward a little.

**GLOVES:** With palms facing the body, slide the right curved open hand down the back of the left open hand a couple of times.

**NEW:** Brush the slightly curved right hand across and over the palm of left hand.

**MY, MINE, OWN:** Place the right flat hand on the chest.

**SHOES:** Tap the sides of the *S* hands together a couple of times.

**THESE, THEM, THEY, THOSE:** Point forward or to the people or objects with the right index finger and move the hand to the right.

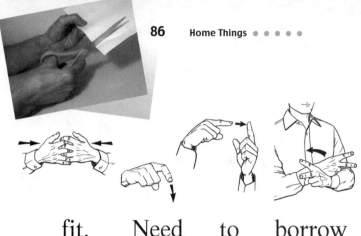

fit.    Need    to    borrow

scissors.    They    lost

● ● ● ● ● ● ● ● ● ● ● ● ● ● ● ● ● ● ● ● ● ● ● ● ● ● ● ● ● ● ● ● ● ● ● ●

**BORROW:** Cross *V* hands in front of the body at the wrists and move them toward self.

**FIT, MATCH:** Interlock the fingers of the curved open hands, palms face body.

**LOST, LOSE:** Touch fingertips of both *and* hands. Then drop them as hands open.

**NEED, HAVE TO, MUST, SHOULD:** Move the right bent index finger down force-

fully several times.

**SCISSORS, CUT:** Open and close the *H* fingers a few times.

**THEY, THESE, THEM, THOSE:** Point forward or to the people or objects with the right index finger and move the hand to the right.

**TO:** Touch the left vertical index fingertip with the right index fingertip.

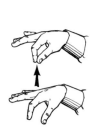

(found)  it.  Search.

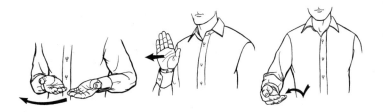

Bring  your  things.

**BRING:** Move both open hands either toward self, another person, or in the direction needed, palms up, with one hand a little ahead of the other.

**FOUND, FIND, DISCOVER:** Place the right hand in front with thumb and index finger separated. Close the thumb and index finger as the hand moves up.

**IT:** Touch the right *I* finger in the flat left palm.

**SEARCH, EXAMINE:** Circle the *C* hand in front of the face a few times.

**THING:** Drop the slightly curved flat hand in front of the body and move it to right.

**YOUR, YOURS, HIS, HER, THEIR:** Push the right flat palm forward toward the person being spoken to.

# Like    your    jacket.

*Use any sign below.*

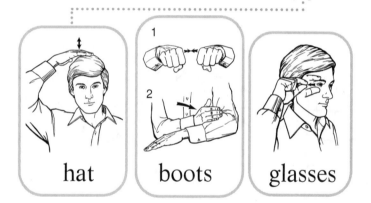

hat        boots        glasses

**BOOTS:** Hit closed hands together twice. Hold right flat hand in bend of left arm.

**GLASSES:** Hold the right *G* hand thumb and index finger near the right eye. Slide them back as they close.

**HAT:** Pat top of head with the right flat hand.

**JACKET, COAT:** Move the *A* hand thumbs down the chest from near the neck.

**LIKE:** Put thumb and index finger of right open hand on chest. Move hand forward, closing thumb and index finger.

**YOUR, YOURS, HIS, HER, THEIR:** Push right flat palm forward toward person being spoken to. If it is not clear from the context, the *male* or *female* sign can be used first. When using *your* in the plural, push right flat palm forward, then move it to right.

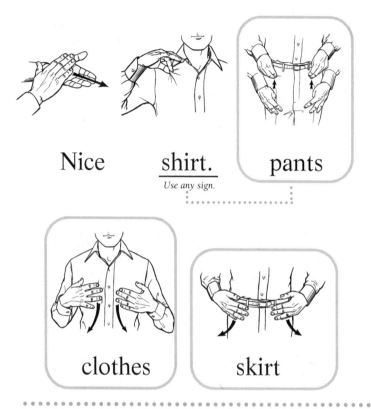

## Nice   shirt.   pants

*Use any sign.*

## clothes   skirt

**CLOTHES, DRESS, WEAR:**
Place the fingertips of the
open hands on the chest.
Then move them down and
repeat.

**NICE, CLEAN:** Pass the right
flat hand over the palm of the
left hand.

**PANTS, SLACKS:** Move the
curved open hands from
below the waist to waist

level ending with *and* hands.

**SHIRT:** Pinch the shirt with
the right thumb and index
finger and pull lightly.

**SKIRT:** Move the flat open
hands down and slightly out-
ward from the waist.

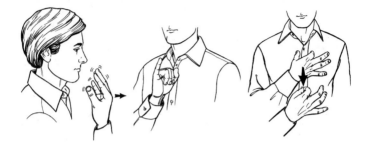

Colors          I          like:

blue          red          white

**BLUE:** Shake the right *B* hand as it moves to the right.

**COLOR:** Wiggle the fingers of the right open hand in front of the mouth as the hand moves forward.

**I:** Place the right *I* hand on the chest, palm left.

**LIKE, ADMIRE:** Hold the thumb and index finger of the right open hand on the chest. Move the hand forward,

closing the thumb and index finger.

**RED:** Move the right index finger down over the lips

**WHITE:** Hold the fingertips of the curved open hand on the chest and move it forward as it closes to an *and* hand.

black

green

purple

pink

yellow

**BLACK:** Move the right index finger across the right eyebrow from left to right.

**GREEN:** Shake the right *G* hand as it moves to the right.

**PINK:** Move the middle finger

of the right *P* hand over the lips.

**PURPLE:** Shake the right *P* hand as it moves to the right.

**YELLOW:** Shake the right *Y* hand as it moves to the right.

Going          home.          I

am          sleepy          (tired).

---

**AM:** Move the right *A* hand thumb forward from the lips.

**GO:** Circle the index fingers around each other as they move forward.

**HOME:** Touch the *and* hand fingertips on the mouth then on the right cheek.

**I:** Place the right *I* hand on the chest, palm left.

**SLEEP, NAP:** Place the

slightly curved open hand in front of the face and bring it down, ending with the *and* hand at the chin.

**TIRED:** Hold both bent hands fingertips on the chest. Swivel the hands down, ending with fingertips pointing up.

# Fun Stuff...

## Match 'em Up

Several items that are needed in the kitchen are signed. Can you match up the pictures with the correct signs? Answers on page 191.

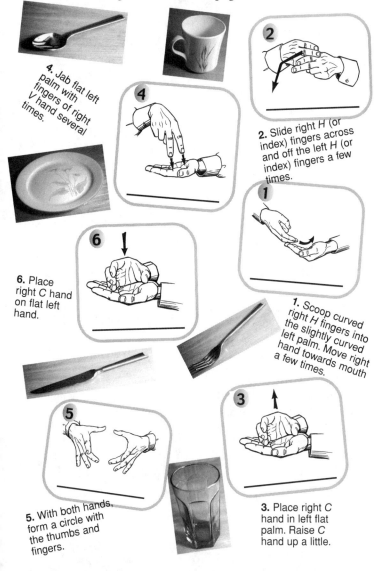

**4.** Jab flat left palm with fingers of right V hand several times.

**2.** Slide right H (or index) fingers across and off the left H (or index) fingers a few times.

**6.** Place right C hand on flat left hand.

**1.** Scoop curved right H fingers into the slightly curved left palm. Move right hand towards mouth a few times.

**5.** With both hands, form a circle with the thumbs and fingers.

**3.** Place right C hand in left flat palm. Raise C hand up a little.

# Try It

Make up sentences using these signs
with others in the book.

dirty      hair      chair

table      soap      mirror

**CHAIR:** Place the right *H* fingers on the left *H* fingers.

**DIRTY:** Wiggle the fingers as the open hand is held palm down under the chin.

**HAIR:** Hold a lock of hair with the right thumb and index fingers.

**MIRROR:** Rotate the slightly curved right hand in front of the face while looking at the palm.

**SOAP:** Rub the right finger-tips across the left flat palm a few times.

**TABLE:** Place the right flat arm and hand on top of the left flat horizontal arm and hand. Right hand can pat left arm.

# Let's Eat 7

I    am    hungry.

*Choose any sign below.*

full    thirsty

**AM:** Move the right *A* hand thumb forward from the lips.

**FULL (physical), FED UP (emotional):** Place the back of the right flat hand under the chin. Emphasize the sign more for *Fed Up.*

**HUNGRY, STARVE:** Move the right *C* hand down the chest.

**I:** Place the right *I* hand on the chest, palm left.

**THIRSTY:** Move the right index finger from under the chin and down the neck.

Breakfast will

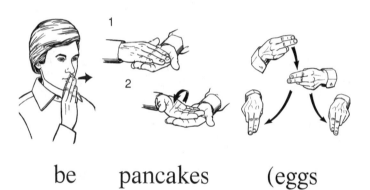

be pancakes (eggs

**BE:** Place right *B* hand at mouth and move it forward.

**BREAKFAST:** Move the fingertips of the right *and* hand to the mouth several times. Next, bend the left arm and rest the left hand in the bend of the right arm. Hold right hand flat and arm bent horizontally. Move right arm upward, palm facing self.

**EGG:** Hit left *H* hand with the right *H* hand; then move both hands down and to the sides.

**PANCAKE, COOK (verb)** With palms facing, place the right hand on the left palm. Flip the right hand over, palm up, and rest it on the left hand.

**WILL (verb), SHALL, WOULD:** Hold the flat hand to right side of face and move it forward.

 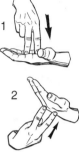 

and     toast).     What

time     do     we

**AND:** Move the open hand to the right as hand closes to all fingertips touching.

**DO, DID, DONE:** Move both *C* hands together to left then to right with palms down.

**TIME, CLOCK, WATCH:** Tap the left wrist a few times with the right curved index finger.

**TOAST:** Push the right *V* fingers into the flat left palm,

then on the back of the left flat hand.

**WE, US:** Circle the right *W* hand from the right side of the chest, palm left, in an arc to the left side of the chest with fingers pointing up. End with palm facing right. Use the *U* hand for *us*.

**WHAT:** Move the tip of the right index finger down across the left flat palm.

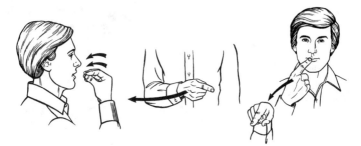

eat?     They     ordered

hamburgers  and   french fries.

• • • • • • • • • • • • • • • • • • • • • • • • • • • • • • • • • • •

**AND:** (*See page 98 at left.*)

**EAT, FOOD, MEAL:** Move the fingertips of the right *and* hand to mouth several times.

**FRENCH FRIES:** Sign *F* and move it to the right.

**HAMBURGER:** Place the right cupped hand on the left cupped hand, then reverse.

**ORDER, COMMAND:** Point to the mouth with the right

index finger. Then quickly twist it forward and slightly down with force.

**THEY, THEM, THESE, THOSE:** Point forward or to the people or objects with the right index finger and move hand to the right.

Some          cake          (pie)

for    dessert?  Don't want.

**CAKE:** Move the right *C* hand fingertips across the left flat hand.

**DESSERT:** Tap both *D* hand fingertips together several times.

**DON'T WANT:** Hold both open curved hands palms up and to the front. Turn them over to palms down.

**FOR:** Place the right index finger at the right temple. Twist it forward as the hand moves forward.

**PIE:** Slide the little finger of the right flat hand over the left flat palm two times, each at different angles.

**SOME:** (*See page at right.*)

More

cookies

and

milk.

- - - - - - - - - - - - - - - - - - - - - - - - - - - - - - - - - - - -

**AND:** Move the open hand to the right as hand closes to all fingertips touching.

**COOKIE:** Place the right *C*-hand thumb and fingertips in the left flat palm, and twist a few times.

**MILK:** Open and close the *S* hands, one after the other, as they move up and down as if milking a cow.

**MORE:** Bring the right *and* hand up to meet the left *and* hand, fingertips touching.

**SOME:** Place the little-finger side of the right curved hand on the left flat palm. Move the right hand toward the body ending with a right flat hand.

My      favorite      fruit

is      <u>banana.</u>      apple

*Use any of the following signs.*

**APPLE:** Touch the right cheek with the right *S* hand extended index finger knuckle. Twist it back and forth.

**BANANA:** Hold up the left index finger. Pretend to be peeling a banana.

**FAVORITE:** Touch the chin a couple times with the right middle finger.

**FRUIT:** Twist the right *F*-hand thumb and index on the right

cheek either forward or backward.

**IS:** Place right *I* hand at the mouth and move it forward.

**MY, MINE, OWN:** Place the right flat hand on the chest.

pear

orange

peach

watermelon

**ORANGE (color and fruit):**
Open and close the right
S hand slightly in front of the
mouth once or twice.

**PEACH:** Place the fingertips
of the right open hand on
the right cheek and move it
down ending with the *and*
hand.

**PEAR:** Place the right hand
over the left *and* hand. Then
slide the right hand off while

closing it into an *and* hand.

**WATERMELON:** Flick the
middle finger of the right
hand against the back of the
closed left hand a few times.

They          had          pizza

for                    lunch

**FOR:** Place the right index finger at the right temple. Twist it forward as the hand moves forward.

**HAD, HAVE, HAS:** Move the bent hands fingertips to the chest.

**LUNCH:** Sign *eat* and *noon*. First move the fingertips of the right *and* hand to the mouth a few times. Then, bend the left arm and hold the left flat hand horizontal. Place the bent vertical right arm elbow on the fingertips of the left hand.

**PIZZA:** Draw a *Z* shape in the air with the right *P* hand.

**THEY, THEM, THESE, THOSE:** Point forward or to the people or objects with the right index finger and move hand to the right.

(supper).    Who    wants

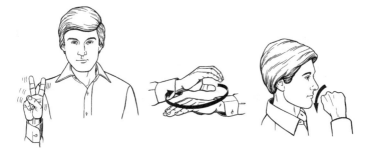

vanilla  (chocolate) ice cream?

• • • • • • • • • • • • • • • • • • • • • • • • • • • • • • • • • • • • • • •

**CHOCOLATE:** Circle right *C* hand over the left flat hand.

**ICE CREAM, LOLLIPOP:** Twist the right *S* hand down near the mouth as if licking an ice cream cone.

**SUPPER, DINNER:** Move the fingertips of right *and* hand to the mouth a few times. Place the right curved hand over the flat horizontal left hand.

**VANILLA:** Shake the right *V* hand back and forth.

**WANT:** Hold both curved open hands with palms up. Move both hands toward the body a few times.

**WHO:** With the right index finger, make a circle in front of the lips.

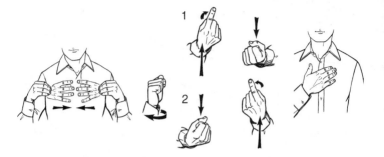

# Microwave the popcorn.  My

# parents     ate     spaghetti

**ATE, FOOD, MEAL:** Move fingertips of right *and* hand to the mouth several times.

**MICROWAVE:** Place both flat *O* hands facing each other at the sides of the chest. Throw the hands towards each other while changing them to curved open hands twice.

**MY, MINE, OWN:** Place the right flat hand on the chest.

**PARENTS:** Touch right temple with right *P* hand middle finger, then right side of chin.

**POPCORN:** Make two *S* hands with palms up. Then flip up the index fingers one after the other.

**SPAGHETTI:** Touch both *I* fingers. Then move them apart as they make little circles.

**THE:** Twist right *T* hand from palm left to palm forward.

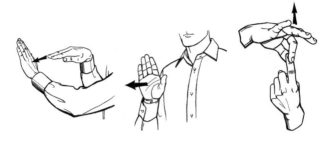

at       their       special

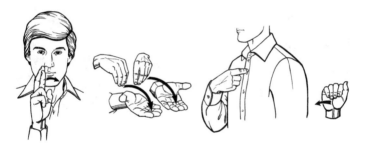

restaurant. Give    me    a

● ● ● ● ● ● ● ● ● ● ● ● ● ● ● ● ● ● ● ● ● ● ● ● ● ● ● ● ● ● ● ● ● ● ● ●

**A:** Move the right *A* hand in a small arc to the right.

**AT:** Touch right flat hand fingertips against back of left flat hand, or fingerspell *A-T*.

**GIVE:** Place the *and* hands in front, palms down. Move hands forward together changing to palms up flat hands.

**ME:** Point to or touch chest with right index finger.

**RESTAURANT:** Place right *R*

hand fingers on right side of mouth then on the left side.

**SPECIAL:** Pull up the left index finger, which is pointing up, with the right thumb and index finger.

**THEIR, HER, HIS:** Push right flat palm forward toward person being spoken to. Sign *male* or *female* first before *his* or *her* if it is not clear from the context.

| sandwich. | Taste | this |

| candy | (gum). | Delicious. |

• • • • • • • • • • • • • • • • • • • • • • • • • • • • • • • • • • • •

**CANDY:** Move the right *U* fingertips down the lips and chin a few times.

**DELICIOUS:** Place the right middle finger on the lips, other fingers extended. Then move the hand forward.

**GUM (chewing)** Place the right *V* fingertips on the cheek. Bend and straighten the *V* fingers a few times.

**SANDWICH:** Put both flat hands together near the mouth.

**TASTE:** Place right middle finger on tip of the tongue, other fingers extended.

**THIS:** Place the right index finger in the left flat palm for something specific.

# *Fun Stuff...*

## Find The Message

Write the name of each sign below. Use the first
letter of each sign to spell out the message at
bottom of page. Answer on page 191.

See page 110.

Message:

\_\_ \_\_ \_\_ **N** \_\_ \_\_ \_\_ \_\_ \_\_ **Y** \_\_ \_\_ **Y**

# Try It

Make up sentences using these signs with others in the book.

drink    water    soda

refrigerator    bread    vegetables

**BREAD:** Place the flat left hand in front of the body. Move the little finger of the right hand down over the back of the left a few times.

**DRINK:** Move the right *C* hand to the mouth as if holding a glass.

**REFRIGERATOR:** Shake both *R* hands with palms facing forward.

**SODA, POP:** Place the right index finger and thumb of the *F* hand into the left *O* hand. Next, hit the left *O* hand with the right open hand.

**VEGETABLE:** Place right *V* index finger, palm forward, on right cheek; twist wrist to left.

**WATER:** Touch the right side of mouth a couple of times with the right *W* index finger.

# Everyday Thoughts & Emotions 8

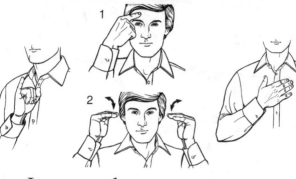

I          hope          my

 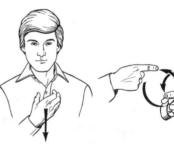

dream          (wish)          comes

**COME:** Circle index fingers as they move toward the body.

**DREAM, DAYDREAM:** Place the right index finger on the forehead. Next, bend and unbend the finger as it moves up and forward.

**FANTASTIC, AWESOME, EXCELLENT:** Push both flat open hands forward and up several times, palms out.

**HOPE:** Touch the forehead with the right index finger. Place flat hands near forehead, palms facing, and bend and unbend them together a couple of times.

**I:** Place the right *I* hand on the chest, palm left.

**MY, MINE, OWN:** Place the right flat hand on the chest.

**WISH:** Move the right *C* hand down the chest.

true.

Love

that.

Fantastic

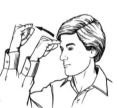

idea.

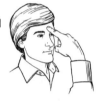

Agree?

• • • • • • • • • • • • • • • • • • • • • • • • • • • • • • • • • •

**AGREE:** Bring the right index finger to the forehead. Place both index fingers together, palms down, and other fingers closed in front of the chest.

**FANTASTIC:** *(See page 112.)*

**IDEA:** Touch the *I* hand finger on the forehead and move it upward, palm in.

**LOVE:** Cross the *S* hands at the wrists over the heart.

**THAT:** Place the right *Y* hand in the left flat palm.

**TRUE, REAL:** Move the right index finger forward in an arc from the lips, palm left.

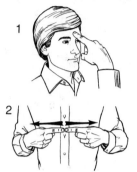

## Disagree.    Which    is

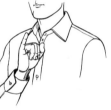

## better?    Choose.    I

**BETTER:** Place the right flat hand fingertips on the mouth. Slide it off to an *A* hand at the right side of the head.

**CHOOSE, PICK:** Hold the open thumb and index finger forward, other fingers extended. Move the hand back as the thumb and index finger touch, as if picking out an item.

**DISAGREE:** Place the right

index finger on the forehead. Next, touch the fingertips of both *D* hands and move them apart quickly.

**I:** Place the right *I* hand on the chest, palm left.

**IS:** Place the right *I* hand at mouth and move it forward.

**WHICH:** Face *A* hand palms in front of chest and apart. Move them alternately up and down.

think          he          likes

you.          Smile.   What's up?

• • • • • • • • • • • • • • • • • • • • • • • • • • • • • • • • • • • • • •

**HE, HIM:** Pretend to be gripping a cap with the right hand. Move it forward a little. Then point the right index finger forward. If the gender is obvious, omit gripping a cap.

**LIKE, ADMIRE:** Hold thumb and index finger of the right open hand on chest. Move the hand forward, closing thumb and index finger.

**SMILE:** Brush fingers of both hands back across the cheeks starting near mouth and smile.

**THINK, CONSIDER:** Circle right index finger at forehead.

**WHAT'S UP?, WHAT'S NEW?:** Place both bent middle fingers of the open hands on the chest. Move hands up the chest and out together.

**YOU:** Point to person you are signing to. Move hand left to right for more than one person.

Keep the secret. Promise.

Why? Because I

**BECAUSE:** Touch the forehead with the right index finger, palm in. Move it slightly up and right to an *A* hand.

**I:** Place the right *I* hand on the chest, palm left.

**KEEP:** Cross the *V* hands at the wrists, right over left.

**PROMISE:** Place the vertical right index finger on the lips. Change the right hand to a flat hand as it moves down to the top of the left *S* hand.

**SECRET, PRIVATE:** Tap the lips with the *A* hand thumb a few times.

**THE:** Hold up the right *T* hand, palm left, and twist it to the right so palm is forward.

**WHY:** Touch the forehead with the right hand fingertips and move it forward changing to a *Y* hand, palm in.

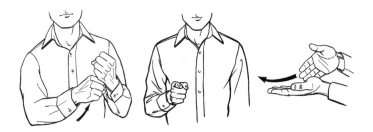

trust        you.        Ok.

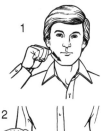

She        is        smart.

● ● ● ● ● ● ● ● ● ● ● ● ● ● ● ● ● ● ● ● ● ● ● ● ● ● ● ● ● ● ● ● ● ● ● ● ● ● ● ● ● ● ●

**IS:** Place right *I* hand at the mouth and move it forward.

**OK, ALL RIGHT:** Slide the edge of the right flat hand forward over the entire left flat hand.

**SHE, HER:** Trace jaw with the right *A*-hand thumb. Then point forward. If the gender is obvious, omit tracing the jaw.

**SMART, BRILLIANT, INTEL-LIGENT:** Touch the forehead with the middle finger of the right open hand. Then turn the hand forward and up.

**TRUST, CONFIDENCE:** Move both hands slightly to the left as they change to *S* hands, the right hand under the left.

**YOU:** Point to person you are signing to. Move hand to right for more than one person.

I   am   <u>happy.</u>

*Use any of the following signs.*

sad    fine    sorry

**AM:** Move the right *A* hand thumb forward from the lips.

**FINE:** Hold the thumb of the right open flat hand on the chest and move it up and forward a little.

**HAPPY:** The right flat hand make a circle as it touches the chest and moves up and out.

**I:** Place the right *I* hand on the chest, palm left.

**SAD:** Place both open hands in front of the face. Drop both hands several inches while looking sad.

**SORRY, APOLOGY, SORROW:** Make a circle over the heart with the right *A* (or *S*) hand.

embarrassed

nervous

mad

surprised

**EMBARRASS, BASHFUL, SHY:** Move the open hands alternately up and down in front of the face, palms in.

**MAD, ANGRY, MOODY:** Bend and unbend the fingers of the right open hand in front of the face a few times.

**NERVOUS:** Shake the open hands in front of the body, palms down.

**SURPRISE:** Hold the closed hands at the sides of the face and flick both index fingers up at the same time.

Remind (show) me.

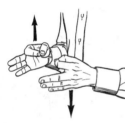  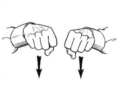

If I can.

**CAN, ABLE, COULD,:** Move both *S* (or *A*) hands down together.

**I:** Place the right *I* hand on the chest, palm left.

**IF:** Move the *F* hands, palms facing, alternately up and down.

**ME:** Point to or touch chest with the right index finger.

**REMIND:** Touch the fore-head with the right *R* hand fingertips.

**SHOW, REVEAL:** Place the right index finger in the left flat palm and move them forward together.

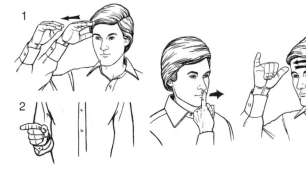

He          is          silly.

Sometimes.   Never.

**HE, HIM:** Pretend to be gripping a cap with the right hand. Move it forward a little. Then point the right index finger forward. If the gender is obvious, omit gripping a cap.

**IS:** Place the right *I* hand at mouth and move it forward.

**NEVER:** Move the right flat hand in a half circle to the right. Then, continue moving the hand quickly away to the right on an angle.

**SILLY, FOOLISH:** With palm left, move the right *Y* hand back and forth in front of the forehead several times.

**SOMETIMES:** Place the right index finger in the left flat palm, which faces right. Move the index finger up and vertical. Pause and repeat action.

# Stop          being          unfair

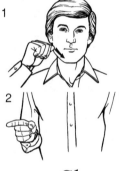

# (jealous).          She          is

---

**BEING:** Place the right *B* hand at the mouth and move it forward.

**IS:** Place the right *I* hand at the mouth and move it forward.

**JEALOUS:** Twist the little finger of the right *J* hand at the right corner of the mouth.

**SHE, HER:** Trace the jaw with the right *A*-hand thumb. Then point forward. If the

gender is obvious, omit tracing the jaw.

**STOP:** Hit the flat left palm with the little finger edge of the right flat hand.

**UNFAIR:** Strike the fingertips of the left *F* hand with the fingertips of right *F* hand.

mean      (selfish).   I doubt it.

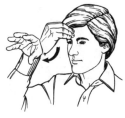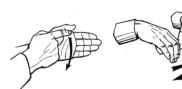

Don't care.    What        do

**DO, DID, DONE:** Move both C hands, palms down, in unison to the left then to the right.

**DON'T CARE:** Touch forehead with the fingertips of the right *and* hand. Twist hand forward as it changes to an open hand.

**I DOUBT IT, DOUBT:** Place the *V* hand before the eyes and bend and unbend the fingers a few times.

**MEAN (adjective), CRUEL:** Move the right bent *V* knuckles down hitting the left bent *V* knuckles.

**WHAT:** Move the tip of the right index finger down across the left flat palm.

**SELFISH, GREEDY:** Place the V fingers forward and pull them back, bending the fingers together.

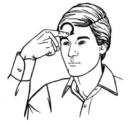

you think? Funny

joke. We laughed.

**FUNNY:** Stroke the tip of the nose with the right *U* fingers a few times.

**JOKE, FOOL (verb):** Hold the bent index finger over the nose and pull head down.

**LAUGH:** Move both extended index fingers from the sides of the mouth up the cheeks a few times.

**THINK:** Circle the right index finger at the forehead.

**WE, US:** Circle the right *W* hand from the right side of the chest, palm left, in an arc to the left side of the chest with fingers pointing up. End with palm facing right. Use the *U* hand for *us*.

**YOU:** Point to the person you are signing to. Move the hand left to right for more than one person.

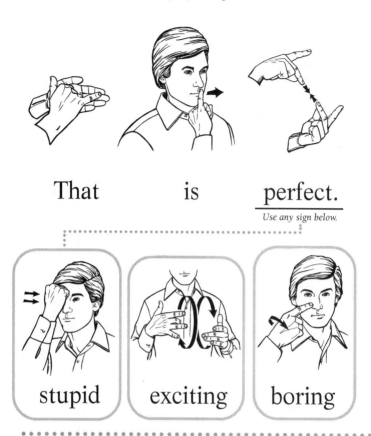

# That          is          perfect.

*Use any sign below.*

stupid          exciting          boring

**BORING:** Place the tip of the index finger on the side of the nose and twist it forward.

**EXCITING, EXCITE:** Brush the middle fingers on the chest with forward circular movements several times with other fingers extended.

**IS:** Place the right *I* hand at the mouth and move it forward.

**PERFECT:** Touch both mid-dle finger *P* hands together.

**STUPID:** Hit the *A* (or *S*) hand, palm in, against the forehead several times.

**THAT:** Place the right *Y* hand in the left palm.

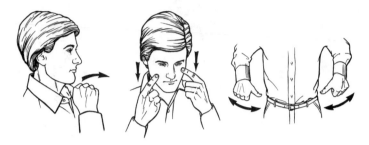

Don't      cry      (brag).

Your fault.    Be    honest.

**BRAG, SHOW OFF:** Hit the sides of the waist with both *A* hand thumbs a few times.

**CRY, TEARS:** Place one or both index fingers under the eyes and move them down the cheeks several times.

**DON'T, DO NOT, DOESN'T, NOT:** Put the *A* hand thumb under the chin. Move it quickly forward.

**HONEST:** Slide right *H* hand middle finger over left flat hand from palm to fingertips.

**ME:** Point to or touch the chest with right index finger.

**YOUR FAULT, MY FAULT, BLAME:** *Blame*-Hit the right *A* hand, with thumb pointing up, on the back of the left closed hand. Then point the right thumb to the person being blamed for *Your Fault* or to yourself for *My Fault*.

# Fun Stuff...

## What Are The Messages?

Several thoughts are signed but the signs are scrambled. Can you figure out the messages? Answers on page 191.

## Try It

Make up sentences using these signs with others in the book.

crazy     hurt     lazy

weird     proud     hate

**CRAZY:** Place the right curved open hand at the temple and twist it back and forth at the wrist.

**HATE:** Flick the middle fingers of both hands out as the hands move forward together.

**HURT (emotion):** Touch the heart with the right middle finger and twist the hand quickly forward and out.

**LAZY:** Place the right L hand, palm in, on the left shoulder once or twice.

**PROUD:** Slide the extended A hand thumb up the chest, palm down.

**WEIRD, STRANGE, ODD:** Twist the right C hand in front of the face.

# Shopping & Going Places 9

Going        to        the        store

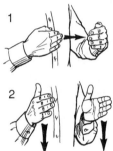  

(neighbors). Count        (add)

**ADD:** Place right open hand to the right, palm down. Place left *and* hand before chest. Move right hand under left while changing it to an *and* hand, ending with fingertips of both *and* hands touching.

**COUNT:** Move the right *F* hand thumb and index finger up the flat vertical left hand.

**GO:** Circle the index fingers around each other as they move forward.

**NEIGHBORS:** Move the right curved hand close to the left curved hand. Then move both flat hands down together, palms facing.

**STORE, SELL, SALE:** Point both *and* hands down. Move them in and out a few times.

**THE:** *(See page 138.)*

**TO:** Touch the left vertical index fingertip with the right index fingertip.

all          your          money.

Save.          We          earned

• • • • • • • • • • • • • • • • • • • • • • • • • • • • • • • • • • • •

**ALL, WHOLE:** Place the left flat hand to the front, palm in. Circle the right flat hand, palm forward, around the left while turning it until it rests in the left palm.

**EARN, COLLECT:** Move right curved hand across the left flat hand. The right hand can end in a closed position.

**MONEY:** Tap the back of the right *and* hand in the left

palm a few times.

**SAVE:** With palms facing in, place inside of *V* fingers on the back of closed left hand.

**WE, US:** Circle the right *W* hand from the right side of the chest, palm left, in an arc to the left side of the chest with fingers pointing up. End with palm facing right. Use the *U* hand for *us*.

**YOUR:** *(See page 88.)*

twenty          dollars,          19

cents          (nothing).          What

● ● ● ● ● ● ● ● ● ● ● ● ● ● ● ● ● ● ● ● ● ● ● ● ● ● ● ● ● ● ● ● ● ● ● ● ● ● ● ●

**CENT, CENTS, PENNY:** Place right index finger on forehead. Then sign the desired number.

**DOLLAR, BILL:** Hold the flat left fingers in the right hand. Pull the right hand off the left hand several times.

**NINETEEN:** Hold the right A hand with thumb up and palm left. Quickly twist the wrist forward while changing to a 9 hand (touching the tips of the thumb and index finger).

**NOTHING:** Hold both O hands in front with palms forward. Move them to the sides in opposite directions while opening both hands together.

**TO:** *(See page 130.)*

**WHAT:** Move the tip of the right index finger down across the left flat palm.

did          you          buy

(pay)?      When?   Yesterday.

● ● ● ● ● ● ● ● ● ● ● ● ● ● ● ● ● ● ● ● ● ● ● ● ● ● ● ● ● ● ● ● ● ● ●

**BUY, PURCHASE:** Place the right *and* hand in the left hand. Next, move it up and forward or to the right.

**DID, DO, DONE:** Move both *C* hands, palms down, in unison to the left then to right.

**PAY:** Place the right index finger in the left flat palm and move the right index finger forward.

**WHEN:** Move the right index finger around the left upright index finger. Then touch the tip of the right index finger on the tip of the left index finger.

**YESTERDAY:** Place the right *Y* (or *A*) hand thumb on the right chin. Move it back toward the ear in an arc.

**YOU:** Point to the person you are signing to. Move the hand left to right for more than one person.

# A    month    (year)    ago.

# That    is    expensive.

*Use any boxed sign.*

• • • • • • • • • • • • • • • • • • • • • • • • • • •

**A:** Move the right *A* hand in a small arc to the right.

**AGO, PAST, WAS, WERE:** With palm facing the body, move the right flat hand backward over the right shoulder. Making sign more slowly and larger means a longer time.

**EXPENSIVE:** Hit back of right *and* hand into left palm. Move the right hand out to the right while opening it.

**IS:** Place right *I* hand at the mouth and move it forward.

**MONTH, MONTHLY:** Move horizontal right index finger down vertical left index finger. For *monthly*, repeat.

**THAT:** Place the right *Y* hand in the left flat palm.

**YEAR:** Rotate the right *S* hand around the left *S* hand, ending with the right hand on the left. Repeat for the plural.

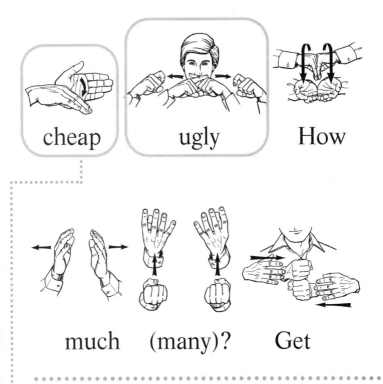

cheap    ugly    How

much   (many)?   Get

**CHEAP, INEXPENSIVE:**
Move the index-finger side of
the right somewhat curved
hand against left flat palm.

**GET:** Move the open hands
together in front of the body
with the right hand on top of
the left, closing to S hands.

**HOW:** Place backs of bent
hands together. Turn them
forward until flat, palms up.

**MANY, LOTS:** Place palm up

S hands in front and throw
them up together into open
hands a couple of times.

**MUCH, LOTS, A LOT:** With
palms facing, hold the open
slightly curved hands in front
and move them apart.

**UGLY:** Cross both index fingers under the nose (other
fingers closed) and pull them
apart to the sides while
bending the index fingers.

 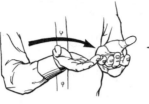 

both.        Carry        this.

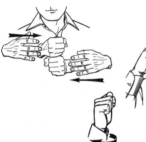  

Get    the    camera.    Take

• • • • • • • • • • • • • • • • • • • • • • • • • • • • • • • • • • • • • •

**BOTH, PAIR:** Draw right *V* fingers down through left *C* hand ending with right *V* fingers touching. Palms face body.

**CAMERA:** Place both open thumb and bent index fingers before the face with all other fingers closed. Move the right index finger up and down.

**CARRY:** Move the slightly curved hands together from right to left (or left to right) in a small arc, palms up.

**GET:** Place curved open hands with palms facing in front of the body. Move them towards each other as they change to *S* hands with the right hand on top of the left.

**TAKE:** Move the open hand from right to left ending with a closed hand near the body.

**THE:** *(See page 138.)*

**THIS:** *(See page 108.)*

## Which Number Is It?

The numbers one through eleven are signed. Can you name them? Some may fool you. Read the directions, then write the number below each sign. Check the answers on page 191. Did you get all of them right?

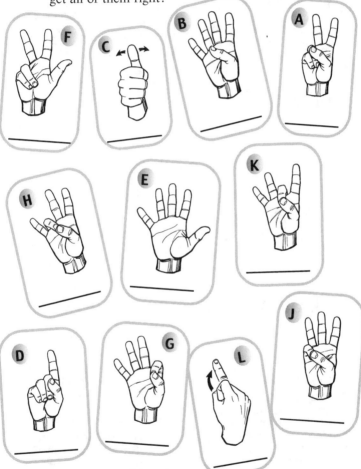

**A, B and D–K.** The right palm faces forward.

**C.** Shake right *A* hand back and forth at wrist with palm facing left, thumb extended up.

**L.** With right *S* hand, palm facing self, flick index finger up.

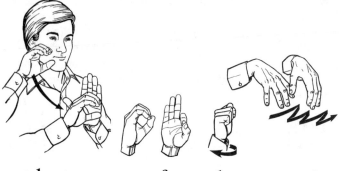

photos          of          the    parade.

Come          here.          Follow

**COME:** Circle index fingers as they move toward body.

**FOLLOW, CHASE:** Hold the *A* hands to the front, right behind left, and move both hands forward together. Sign *chase* more rapidly.

**HERE:** Move both flat hands, palms up, in opposite forward circles in front of the body. Or point down in front of the right side of the body.

**PARADE:** Place the bent left open hand in front of the right bent open hand. Swing them from side to side as both hands move forward.

**PHOTOS, PHOTOGRAPH, PICTURE:** Move the right *C* hand from the right cheek and place it against left vertical flat hand.

**THE:** Twist right *T* hand from palm left to palm forward.

us.    Which    way?

Stay    with    me.

**ME:** Point to or touch the chest with right index finger.

**STAY, REMAIN:** Place the right *A* thumbtip on left *A* thumbtip. Push them down together.

**US, WE:** Circle the right *U* hand from the right side of the chest, palm left, in an arc to the left side of the chest with fingers pointing up. End with palm facing right. Use the *W* hand for *we*.

**WAY, STREET, AVENUE, HIGHWAY, PATH, ROAD:** Face both flat hands palm to palm and move them forward in a winding movement.

**WHICH:** Face the *A* hands palm to palm in front of the chest and move them alternately up and down.

**WITH:** Place both *A* hands together, palms facing.

Walk      slow.      How

far?    Grandmother    and

- - - - - - - - - - - - - - - - - - - - - - - - - - - - - - - - - - - - - - - - - - -

**AND:** Move the open hand to the right as hand closes to all fingertips touching.

**FAR, DISTANT:** Place the *A* hands together, palms facing, and move the right hand forward.

**GRANDMOTHER:** Touch the chin with the thumb of the right open hand. Move it forward in two small arcs.

**HOW:** Place both bent hands together back to back. Turn them forward until the hands are flat, palms up.

**SLOW:** Slide the right hand slowly over the back of the left hand from fingertips to wrist.

**WALK, STEP:** Imitate walking by placing both flat hands palms down and alternately moving each hand forward.

Grandfather    visit    for

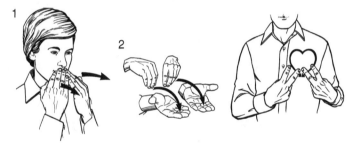

Thanksgiving    (Valentines).

**FOR:** Place the right index finger at the right temple. Twist it forward as the hand moves forward.

**GRANDFATHER:** Touch the thumb of the open hand on the forehead. Move it forward in two small arcs.

**THANKSGIVING:** Bring the fingertips of both flat hands to the lips. Move the hands forward until palms are up.

(One hand can be used). Place the *and* hands in front, palms down, and move them forward together changing to palms up flat hands.

**VALENTINE:** Draw a heart shape over the heart with the *V* hands.

**VISIT:** Place both *V* hands up, palms in, and move them in alternating forward circles.

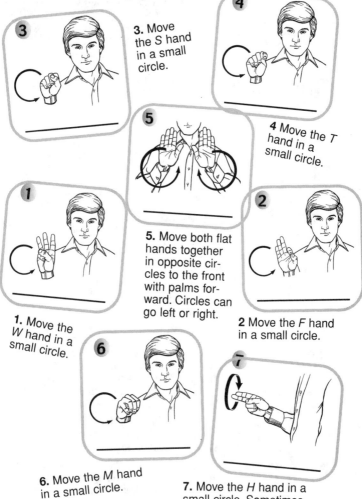

# Fun Stuff...

## Which Day Is It?

The days of the week are signed. Can you guess each one? Two may fool you. Read directions, then write the name below each sign. That initialized hand shape is a good hint. See answers on page 191.

**3.** Move the S hand in a small circle.

**4** Move the T hand in a small circle.

**5.** Move both flat hands together in opposite circles to the front with palms forward. Circles can go left or right.

**1.** Move the W hand in a small circle.

**2** Move the F hand in a small circle.

**6.** Move the M hand in a small circle.

**7.** Move the H hand in a small circle. Sometimes signed with a T and H.

Get out    of    the    car.

Get in.    Where    is

- - - - - - - - - - - - - - - - - - - - - - - - - - - - - - - - - -

**CAR, DRIVE:** Make two *S* hands. Pretend to be steering a car.

**GET IN:** Place the curved *V* fingers into the left *O* hand.

**GET OUT:** Take the curved *V* fingers out of the left *O* hand.

**IS:** Place right *I* hand at the mouth and move it forward.

**OF:** Fingerspell *O-F* near the right shoulder.

**THE:** Hold up the right *T* hand, palm left, and twist it to the right so palm is forward.

**WHERE:** Point the right index finger up and shake it back and forth quickly.

the   restroom.   Go   <u>right.</u>

*Choose any sign below.*

left        up        down

**DOWN:** Point down with the right index finger; move hand down a little.

**GO:** Circle the index fingers around each other as they move forward.

**LEFT (direction):** Move the *right L* hand to the left with palm forward.

**RESTROOM:** Move the right *R* hand to right in a small arc.

**RIGHT (direction):** Move the *R* hand, palm forward, to the right.

**THE:** Twist the right *T* hand to the right from a palm-left position.

**UP:** Point up with the right index finger and move hand up a little.

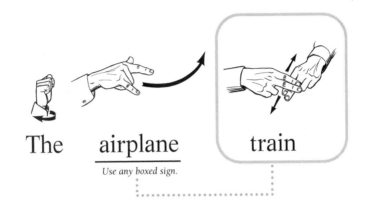

The  _airplane_  train

_Use any boxed sign._

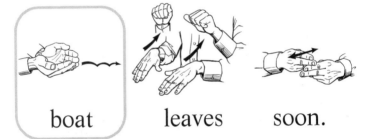

boat  leaves  soon.

**AIRPLANE, FLY, JET:** Move the *Y* hand, with index finger extended, forward and up.

**BOAT, BOATING:** Move both cupped hands forward in a bouncing motion.

**LEAVE:** Hold both flat hands to the right, palms down, and draw them up to self, ending in *A* hands.

**SOON, SHORT (length or time):** Cross the *H* hands and slide, back and forth, the right fingers over the left.

**THE:** Twist right *T* hand from palm left to palm forward.

**TRAIN, RAILROAD:** Move the right *H* fingers over the left *H* fingers, palms down, several times.

Wait a second (minute).

Hurry. Let's go

• • • • • • • • • • • • • • • • • • • • • • • • • • • • • • • • • • • • •

**A:** *(See page 134.)*

**GO:** Circle the index fingers around each other as they move forward.

**HURRY, RUSH:** Quickly move the *H* hand up and down in a forward movement.

**LET'S, LET US:** Face both *L* hands in front, palms facing, and apart. Move them together so fingers point slightly up.

**MINUTE:** Place the *D* hand index finger against the vertical left flat palm which faces right. Move the right index finger past the left little finger.

**SECOND, MOMENT (time):** Place the right *1* hand against the vertical flat left hand. Move the index finger forward a little in a short arc.

**WAIT:** Face curved open hands to left, palms up, right behind left; wiggle fingers.

shopping

now.
*Use any sign.*

someday

early      morning      afternoon

**AFTERNOON:** Hold the right forearm at a 45-degree angle on back of left flat hand which is horizontal and palm down.

**EARLY:** Slide the right curved middle finger over the back of the left closed hand.

**NOW, IMMEDIATE:** Quickly drop bent (or Y) hands in front of body at waist, palms up.

**MORNING:** Bend the left arm and rest the left hand in the bend of the right arm. Hold the right hand flat and arm bent horizontally. Move right arm upright, palm facing self.

**SHOPPING, SHOP (noun and verb):** Place the right *and* hand in the left hand. Move it up and forward or to the right several times.

**SOMEDAY, FUTURE:** Move right flat hand forward in an arc from right side of head.

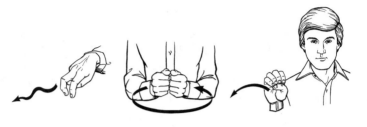

Travel together. Easter

vacation. Where are

**ARE:** Move the *R* hand forward from the lips.

**CITY, TOWN, VILLAGE:** Touch both flat hand fingertips together forming a triangle. Repeat a couple of times as hands move to the right.

**EASTER:** With palm forward move the right *E* hand in a small arc to the right.

**TOGETHER:** Hold the *A* hands together, palms facing, and circle them from right to left.

**TRAVEL, JOURNEY, TRIP:** Move the curved *V* hand in a forward wavy movement, palm down.

**VACATION, HOLIDAY:** Place the thumbs at or near the arm pits and wiggle fingers.

**WHERE:** Point the right index finger up and shake it back and forth quickly.

you          from?          California.

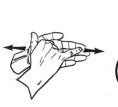

Mexico.  New York.    Europe.

**CALIFORNIA, GOLD:** Touch the right ear with the right index finger. Bring the *Y* hand forward and shake it.

**EUROPE:** Move the right *E* hand in a small circle, at the right side of the head, palm out.

**FROM:** Touch the right *X* index finger on the left vertical index finger and move it back and away.

**MEXICO, MEXICAN:** Slide the right *M* hand fingertips down the right cheek a couple of times. Add *Person Ending* for *Mexican* person.

**NEW YORK:** Slide the right *Y* hand back and forth on the left flat hand.

**YOU:** Point to the person you are signing to. Move the hand left to right for more than one person.

## Try It
Make up sentences using these signs
with others in the book.

America    spend    country

city    last    state

**AMERICA, AMERICAN:**
Interlock the slightly curved
open hands. Move them in a
circle from right to left. Add
the *person ending* sign when
using *American* in reference
to a person.

**CITY:** *(See page 148.)*

**COUNTRY (national territory):** Rub right *Y* hand, palm
in, in a circle near left elbow.

**LAST, FINAL, END:** Strike

the left little finger with the
right index finger. Both little
fingers can be used.

**SPEND:** Place back of right
*and* hand into left flat palm.
Open right hand as it slides
off the fingertips of the left.

**STATE (geographical):** Move
the *S* hand down the left flat
hand from fingers to palm.

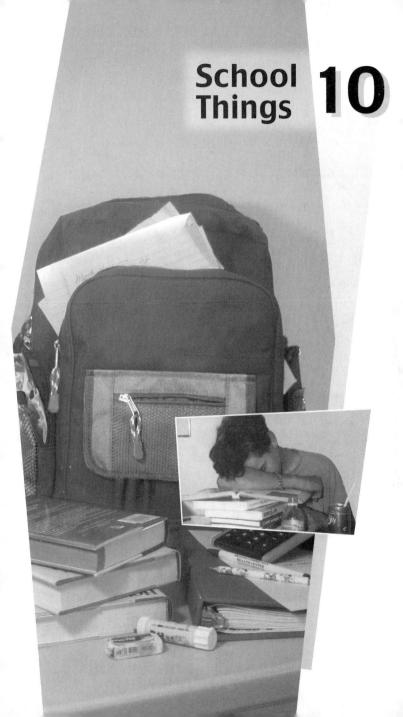

# School Things

**10**

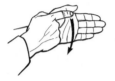

What

school

do

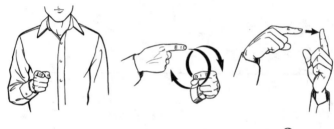

you

go

to?

**DO, DID, DONE:** Move both *C* hands together to the left then to the right, palms down.

**GO:** Circle the index fingers around each other as they move forward.

**SCHOOL:** Clap the hands two times.

**TO:** Touch the left vertical index fingertip with the right index fingertip.

**WHAT:** Move the tip of the right index finger down across the left flat palm.

**YOU:** Point to the person you are signing to. Move the hand left to right for more than one person.

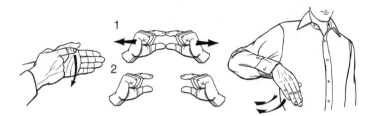

What    grade?    Late

for    practice.    My

**FOR:** Place the right index finger at the right temple. Twist it forward as the hand moves forward.

**GRADE:** Touch fingertips and thumbs of both modified *G* hands with palms facing out, then move hands apart.

**LATE, NOT YET:** Move the right flat hand back and forth a few times near the right side.

**MY, MINE, OWN:** Place the right flat hand on the chest.

**PRACTICE:** Move the *A* hand knuckles back and forth over the left index finger.

**WHAT:** Move the tip of the right index finger down across the left flat palm.

homework        is        done.

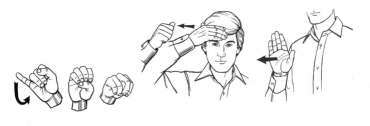

Jen        forgot        her

**ANN:** Fingerspell *A-N-N*.

**DONE, FINISH, COMPLETE:** Place the open hands in front, palms facing the body and fingers pointing up. Twist them to the sides several times.

**FORGOT, FORGET:** Move the right open hand, palm in, across forehead from left to right ending with *A* hand to the right side of head.

**HER, HIS, THEIR, YOUR,**

**YOURS (singular):** Push the right flat hand, palm forward, toward the person or persons you are referring to. Sign *male* or *female* first if gender is not obvious from context.

**HOMEWORK:** Touch the *and* hand fingertips on mouth then on right cheek. Tap right *S* hand wrist on left *S* hand wrist several times, palms down.

**IS:** *(See page 155 at right.)*

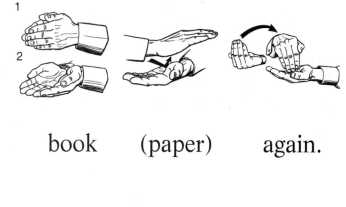

book        (paper)        again.

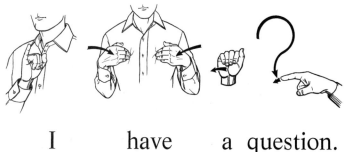

I        have        a question.

**A:** Move the right *A* hand in a small arc to the right.

**AGAIN, REPEAT:** Turn the bent right hand up and into the left flat palm.

**BOOK:** Close both flat hands palm to palm, then open them.

**HAVE, HAD, HAS:** Move the bent hands fingertips to the chest.

**I:** Place the right *I* hand on the chest, palm left.

**IS:** Place right *I* hand at the mouth and move it forward.

**PAPER:** Hit the heel of the right flat hand against the heel of the left flat hand two times from right to left.

**QUESTION, QUESTION MARK:** Draw a question mark in the air with the right index finger. Include the period.

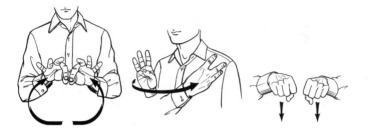

Important.          We          can

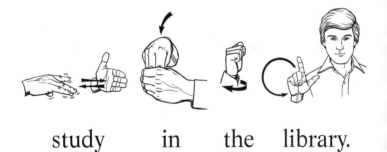

study        in        the      library.

● ● ● ● ● ● ● ● ● ● ● ● ● ● ● ● ● ● ● ● ● ● ● ● ● ● ● ● ● ● ● ● ●

**CAN, COULD:** Move both *S* (or *A*) hands down together.

**IN:** Place the right *and* hand fingertips into the left *C* hand.

**IMPORTANT:** Move the *F* hands in a circle, from palms up to palms down to the center of body until fingers touch.

**LIBRARY:** Move the right *L* hand to the right in a small circle, palm forward.

**STUDY:** Wiggle the fingers of the right open hand as the hand moves back and forth in front of the left flat hand.

**THE:** Twist right *T* hand from palm left to palm forward.

**WE, US:** Circle the right *W* hand from the right side of the chest, palm left, in an arc to the left side of the chest with fingers pointing up. End with palm facing right. Use the *U* hand for *us*.

  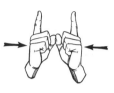

## Whisper.    Listen.    Meet

## me        after        school.

**AFTER (time):** Move the slightly curved right hand forward and away from the sightly curved left hand.

**LISTEN, HEAR:** Cup the right *C* hand behind the right ear. Turn head to left a little.

**ME:** Point to or touch the chest with right index finger.

**MEET:** Extend the index fingers of both hands and hold them at the sides with palms facing. Bring both hands together.

**SCHOOL:** Clap the hands two times.

**WHISPER:** With palm facing left, place the curved flat hand at the right side of the mouth. Lean forward or to the side.

I       want       to

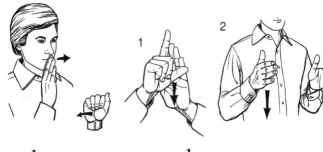

be    a     lawyer.

*Use any sign.*

**A:** Move the right *A* hand in a small arc to the right.

**BE:** Place the right *B* hand at the mouth and move it forward.

**I:** Place the right *I* hand on the chest, palm left.

**LAWYER, ATTORNEY:** Place the right *L* hand on the vertical left flat fingers and move the *L* hand down to the palm. Sign *person ending* by placing both flat hands to the front and apart. Move them down together.

**TO:** Touch the left vertical index fingertip with the right index fingertip.

**WANT:** Hold both curved open hands with palms up. Move both hands toward the body a few times.

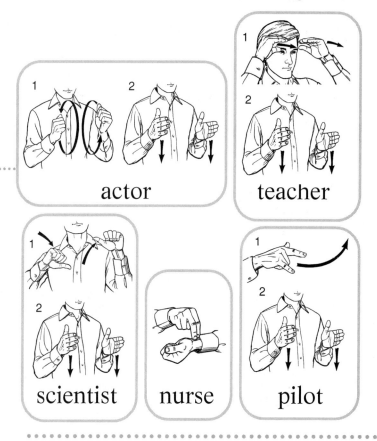

actor

teacher

scientist

nurse

pilot

**ACTOR, ACTRESS** Move the A hands, palms facing, in alternate circles toward the body. Place both flat hands to the front and apart. Move them down together.

**NURSE:** Hold the extended fingertips of the right N hand on pulse area of left wrist.

**PILOT:** Move Y hand, with index finger extended, forward and up. Place both flat hands to the front and apart. Move them down together.

**SCIENTIST:** Move the extended A hand thumbs alternately in and down a few times in front of the chest.

**TEACHER:** Place both open *and* hands in front of forehead facing each other. Move them forward ending with *and* hands. Place flat hands to front and move them down together.

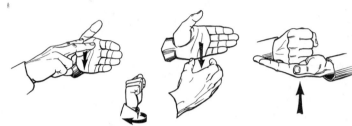

Read    the    chapter?    Help.

Explain         this.         Don't

**CHAPTER:** Slide the right *C* hand thumb and fingers down the horizontal left palm.

**DON'T, DO NOT, NOT:** Put the *A* hand thumb under the chin. Move it quickly forward.

**EXPLAIN:** Hold the *F* hands to the front, palms facing, and close together. Move them alternately back and forth.

**HELP:** Lift the right *S* hand with the left flat hand.

**READ:** Point the right *V* fingers at the left flat hand and move the *V* hand down.

**THE:** Twist right *T* hand from palm left to palm forward.

**THIS:** Place the right index finger in the left flat palm for something specific.

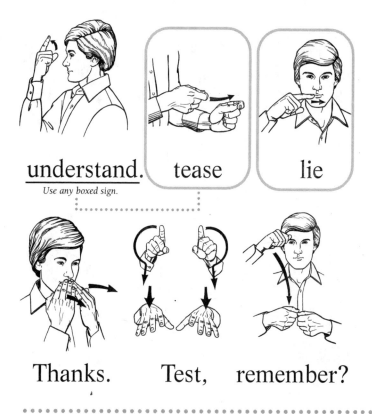

understand.
*Use any boxed sign.*

tease

lie

Thanks.

Test,

remember?

**LIE:** Push right index finger across lips from right to left.

**REMEMBER:** Place the right A hand thumb on the forehead then on the left A hand thumb.

**TEASE:** Move the right modified A hand knuckles over the left modified A hand.

**TEST, QUIZ:** Draw opposite question marks in the air with both index fingers. Open and

move both hands forward.

**THANKS, YOU'RE WELCOME:** Smile and bring fingertips of both flat hands to lips. Move the hands forward until palms are up. One hand can be used.

**UNDERSTAND:** Flick up the index finger in front of the forehead, palm in.

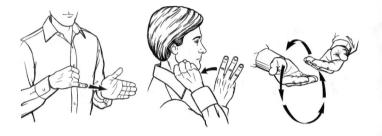

It            was            easy

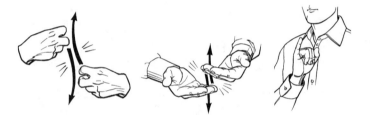

(hard).    Doesn't matter.    I
difficult

**DOESN'T MATTER, ANY-HOW:** Move the fingertips of both slightly curved hands up and down over each other several times with palms up.

**EASY, SIMPLE:** Place the left curved hand in front with palm up. Move the right curved hand up several times brushing the little-finger side against the fingertips of the left hand.

**HARD, DIFFICULT:** Hit the bent *V* hand knuckles as the hands move up and down.

**I:** Place the right *I* hand on the chest, palm left.

**IT:** Touch the right *I* finger in the flat left palm.

**WAS:** Move the *W* hand backward near the right cheek and close it to an *S* hand.

passed    (failed).    Someone

  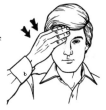

cheated.    I    know.

● ● ● ● ● ● ● ● ● ● ● ● ● ● ● ● ● ● ● ● ● ● ● ● ● ● ● ● ● ● ● ● ● ● ● ● ● ● ●

**CHEAT:** Face the left *Y* hand forward with the index finger extended and palm down. Make the same handshape with the right hand and slide it back and forth over the top of the left hand several times.

**FAIL:** Place right *V* hand in left flat hand, palms up. Slide it off and down a little.

**I:** Place the right *I* hand on the chest, palm left.

**KNOW, INTELLIGENCE, KNOWLEDGE:** Touch the fingertips of the right hand on the forehead several times.

**PASS:** Hold *A* hands with right slightly behind left. Move the right hand ahead of left.

**SOMEONE, SOMEBODY, SOMETHING:** Hold the right index finger up, palm facing forward. Shake it slightly back and forth from left to right.

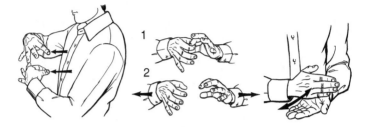

Interesting          story.          Share

 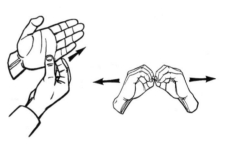

your          magazine.          No

**INTERESTING, INTEREST:**
Hold both hands with open
index fingers and thumbs on
the chest, other fingers
extended, right above left.
Move them forward closing
the thumb and index fingers.

**MAGAZINE:** Grasp the bottom edge of the left flat hand
between the right index finger and thumb. Slide the right
hand along the left hand's
edge and little finger.

**NO, NONE:** Place *O* hands to
front, fingers touching. Move
apart in opposite directions.

**SHARE:** Slide the little-finger
edge of the right flat hand
back and forth on the left flat
hand from wrist to fingertips
a couple times.

**STORY:** Join the *F* hand fingers like two links. Separate
them to the sides a few times.

**YOUR:** *(See page 179.)*

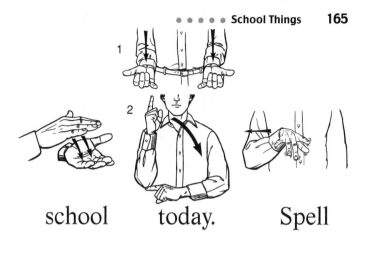

school            today.            Spell

that            word.            Right.

**RIGHT, CORRECT:** Face the index fingers forward with right above left and bring right hand down on left hand.

**SCHOOL:** Clap the hands two times.

**SPELL, FINGERSPELL:** Move fingers up and down as right open hand moves from left to right with palm down.

**THAT:** Place the right Y hand in the left flat palm.

**TODAY:** Move both Y (or flat) hands down, palms up, at the same time. Hold left arm flat, index finger pointing right. Place the elbow of the bent right arm on the left index finger. Move the right arm, index finger up, across the body in a short arc.

**WORD:** Place the Q fingertips on the vertical left index finger which faces palm left.

 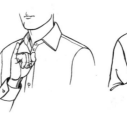 

Wrong.      I      like

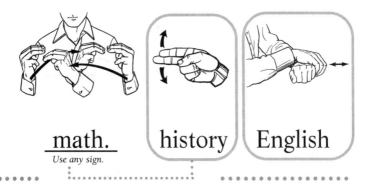

math.     history     English
*Use any sign.*

**ENGLISH, ENGLAND:** Hold the left closed hand at the wrist with the right curved hand and move them forward and back. Add the *person ending* sign when using *English* in reference to a person.

**HISTORY:** Swing the *H* hand up and down a little.

**I:** Place the right *I* hand on the chest, palm left.

**LIKE, ADMIRE:** Hold the thumb and index finger of the right open hand on the chest. Move the hand forward, closing the thumb and index finger.

**MATH, MATHEMATICS:** Hold the *M* hands with palms facing and cross the hands, right behind left.

**WRONG:** Hold the *Y* hand on the chin, palm in.

# Fun Stuff...

## Are They Opposite?

Two signs are placed in each box. Are they
opposite in meaning? Answer "yes" or "no",
then see answers on page 191.

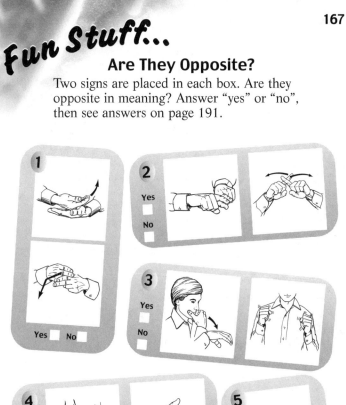

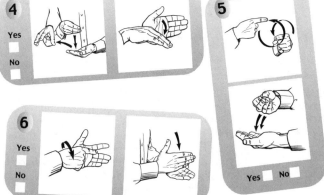

# Try It

Make up sentences using these signs with others in the book.

cafeteria    dictionary    famous

write    gossip    make

**CAFETERIA:** With palm facing left, place the right *C* hand (index finger side) on the right side of the mouth then on the left side of the mouth.

**DICTIONARY:** Shake the right *D* hand, palm forward.

**GOSSIP:** Open and close the *Q* fingers and thumbs near the mouth a few times.

**MAKE:** Hit the left *S* hand with the right *S* hand. Twist the hands in. Then repeat.

**SUBJECT, QUOTE, TITLE:** Place the curved *V* hands in front, palms forward, and twist them to palms facing each other.

**WRITE:** Pretend to be writing on the left flat palm with the right index finger and thumb.

# Technology
# & Science 11

Tod          is          getting          a

computer          and          scanner.

● ● ● ● ● ● ● ● ● ● ● ● ● ● ● ● ● ● ● ● ● ● ● ● ● ● ● ● ● ● ● ● ● ●

**A:** Move the right *A* hand in a small arc to the right.

**AND:** Move the open hand to the right as hand closes to all fingertips touching.

**COMPUTER:** With the right *C* hand, make a double arc from right to left in front of the forehead.

**GET:** Move the open hands together in front of the body with the right hand on top of

the left, forming *S* hands.

**IS:** Place the right *I* hand at the mouth and move it forward.

**SCANNER:** With palm facing left, move the right *X* hand back and forth two times under the palm-down left flat horizontal hand.

**TOD:** Fingerspell *T-O-D* near the right shoulder.

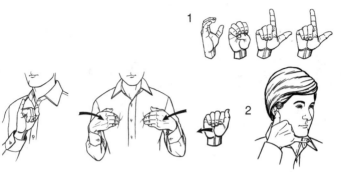

I    have    a    cell phone.

My          sister          bought

**A:** Move the right *A* hand in a small arc to the right.

**BOUGHT, BUY, PURCHASE:** Place the right *and* hand in the left hand. Move it up and forward or to the right.

**CELL PHONE:** Fingerspell *C-E-L-L* near the right shoulder. Then position the *Y* hand at the right of the face so that the thumb is near the ear and little finger near mouth.

**HAVE, HAS, HAD:** Move the bent hands fingertips to the chest.

**I:** Place the right *I* hand on the chest, palm left.

**MY, MINE, OWN:** Place the right flat hand on the chest.

**SISTER:** Slide the thumb of the extended *A* hand along the right side of the jaw. Place both index fingers together.

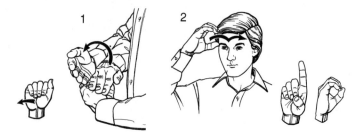

a      laptop computer.      Do

you        BLOG?        Printer

● ● ● ● ● ● ● ● ● ● ● ● ● ● ● ● ● ● ● ● ● ● ● ● ● ● ● ● ● ●

**A:** *(See page 173 at right.)*

**BLOG:** Fingerspell *B-L-O-G* near the right shoulder.

**DO:** Fingerspell *D-O*.

**LAPTOP COMPUTER, NOTEBOOK COMPUTER:** Place right flat hand on left flat hand, palms facing, fingers pointing in opposite directions; twist right hand up while still making contact with right little finger on left palm.

Move right *C* hand across forehead in two arcs from right to left, palm left.

**PRINTER (machine):** Move right index finger and thumb together as though picking something up; then place them on left flat palm.

**YOU:** Point to person you are signing to. Move hand left to right for more than one person.

problem.      Surf the net

with      me.

• • • • • • • • • • • • • • • • • • • • • • • • • • • • • • • • • • •

**A:** Move the right *A* hand in a small arc to the right.

**ME:** Point to or touch the chest with right index finger.

**PROBLEM:** Twist the bent *U* (or *V*) hand knuckles back and forth in opposite directions.

**SURF THE NET, SURF:** Make a few circular motions across the face from right to left with the right *C* hand, palm left. Move the extended right index finger, which points forward with palm down, in a wavy movement from under the left flat hand as the left flat palm moves up the right arm.

**WITH:** Place both *A* hands together, palms facing.

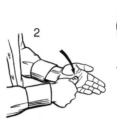

E-mail    later.

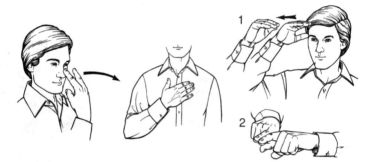

See    my    brother's

---

**BROTHER:** Place the right flattened *C* hand at the forehead and close fingers. Hand can move forward a little. Place index fingers together.

**E-MAIL (Electronic Mail):** Fingerspell *E* near the right shoulder. Next, place the right *A* thumb on the mouth and then on the palm of the upturned left hand.

**LATER, AFTER A WHILE:** Hold the right *L* hand in vertical left palm and twist it forward and down.

**MY, MINE, OWN:** Place the right flat hand on the chest.

**SEE, SIGHT, VISION:** Point right *V* fingertips toward the eyes. Move the hand forward.

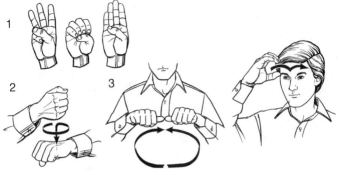

web site.          Computer

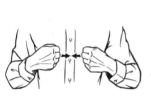

crashed.          Call          me

Telephone

**CALL, TELEPHONE:** Hold thumb of right *Y* hand to ear.

**COMPUTER:** With the right *C* hand, make a double arc from right to left in front of the forehead, palm left.

**CRASH, ACCIDENT, WRECK:** Hit both *S* hands head on.

**ME:** Point to or touch the chest with the right index finger.

**WEB SITE:** 1. Fingerspell *W-E-B*.

2. Make a circle with right *A* hand, palm left, above the left closed hand, palm down; place right *A* hand on left. 3. With palms down, touch the thumbs of both *A* hands together a short distance in front of the chest. Circle both hands toward self and touch thumbs again near chest.

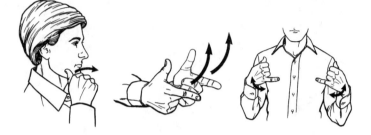

tomorrow.    Let's    play

video games.    Turn

• • • • • • • • • • • • • • • • • • • • • • • • • • • • • • • •

**LET'S, LET US:** Face both *L* hands to the front with palms facing each other and several inches apart. Then move them up together.

**PLAY, RECREATION:** Hold up the *Y* hands. Shake them back and forth at the wrists.

**TOMORROW:** Place the right *A* thumb on the right cheek or chin area and move it forward in an arc.

**TURN:** Rotate the index fingers in right to left circles around each other with the right pointing down and left pointing up.

**VIDEO GAME:** Hold both *A* hands to the front and side by side and alternately move the thumbs up and down.

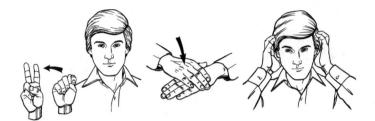

| TV | on. | Radio |
|---|---|---|

| (VCR) | off. | Where |
|---|---|---|

● ● ● ● ● ● ● ● ● ● ● ● ● ● ● ● ● ● ● ● ● ● ● ● ● ● ● ● ● ● ● ● ● ● ● ● ● ● ● ●

**OFF:** Move the flat right hand up a few inches off the back of the flat left hand, palms down.

**ON:** Place the right flat hand on top of the left flat hand, palms down.

**RADIO:** Place the cupped hands over the ears.

**TELEVISION:** Fingerspell *T-V.*

**VCR:** Fingerspell *V-C-R.*

**WHERE:** Point the right index finger up and shake it quickly back and forth.

is the remote control?

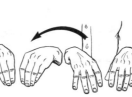

Don't know.          Put          a

**A:** Move the right *A* hand in a small arc to the right.

**DON'T KNOW, DIDN'T RECOGNIZE:** Touch the fingertips of the right flat hand on the forehead and flip the hand as it moves forward a little, palm out.

**IS:** Place right *I* hand at the mouth and move it forward.

**PUT, MOVE:** Hold the open curved hands to the left front, palms down. Move them together up and down to the right while closing them to *and* hands.

**REMOTE CONTROL:** Point the extended right *A* hand thumb forward, palm left, and move the thumb up and down a few times.

**THE:** Hold up the right *T* hand, palm left, and twist it to the right so palm is forward.

disk    in.    Is    your

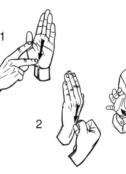

science    project    finished?

**DISK, DISKETTE:**
Place the right *D* hand, palm down with index pointing forward, on the left flat hand, palm up, and circle twice.

**FINISH, COMPLETE:** Open hands in front, palms face in and fingers pointing up, twist them to sides several times.

**IN:** Place right *and* hand fingertips into the left *C* hand.

**IS:** *(See page 178 at left.)*

**SCIENCE, EXPERIMENT:**
Move extended *A* hand thumbs alternately in and down a few times in front of the chest. Use *E* hands for *experiment*.

**YOUR, YOURS, HIS, HER, THEIR:** Push right flat palm forward toward person. Sign *male* or *female* first if it is not clear from the context. When *your* is plural, push right flat palm forward and to right.

Almost.　　This　　electric

magnet　　is　　very

- - - - - - - - - - - - - - - - - - - - - - - - - - - - - - - - - - - - -

**ALMOST:** With both palms up, move the little-finger edge of the right hand up hitting the fingertips of the left curved hand.

**ELECTRICITY, BATTERY:** With other fingers closed, tap the bent index and middle fingers against each other several times. Index fingers only can be used.

**IS:** Place right *I* hand at the mouth and move it forward.

**MAGNET, MAGNETIC:** With palms down, place both *M* hands to front of chest and a few inches apart; twist hands towards each other until index fingers (or fingertips) touch once or twice

**THIS:** Put right index finger in left flat palm for something specific.

**VERY:** *(See page at right.)*

strong.          See          my

IPOD.          Great    graphics.

**GRAPHICS:** Draw a wavy line with little-finger side of right *G* hand over left flat palm.

**GREAT, EXCELLENT, FAN-TASTIC:** Push both flat open hands forward and up several times, palms out.

**IPOD:** Fingerspell *I-P-O-D.*

**MY, MINE, OWN:** Place the right flat hand on the chest.

**SEE, SIGHT, VISION:** Point right *V* fingertips toward eyes.

Then move the hand forward.

**STRONG, POWERFUL:** Bend the left arm and draw an arc over the left biceps with the right curved hand.

**VERY:** Place both *V* hand fingertips together and move them apart.

# Let's Sing...

## If You're Happy

Here is a song to teach your younger brother, sister, or a friend. Signing a song is a good way to learn to sign.

If    you're    happy    and    you

know    it,    clap    your    hands.

If    you're    happy    and    you

know    it,    clap    your    hands.

If you're happy and you

know it, then your face

   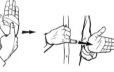

will sure - ly show it.

If you're happy and you

 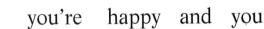

know it, clap your hands.

## Try It

Make up sentences using these signs with others in the book.

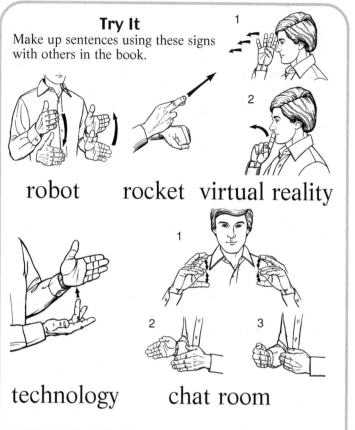

robot    rocket    virtual reality

technology    chat room

**CHAT ROOM:** With flattened C hands at upper chest, palms facing, close and open them together a couple of times. Place both flat hands in front, palms facing; move left hand near body and right hand in front, palms facing body.
**ROBOT:** Place flat hands at each side, right higher than left. Move arms up and down alternately like a *robot*.
**ROCKET:** Place right R hand on back of left S hand and move it up on an angle.
**TECHNOLOGY:** Tap tip of bent palm-up-middle finger of right open hand twice on little-finger edge of left flat hand.
**VIRTUAL REALITY:** Touch the right side of forehead with right index finger of right 4 hand, palm left. Move right hand forward in several short movements. Move right index finger in an arc from lips.

# Answers

## Ch. 2, page 36
## Which Animal Is It?

1. Elephant
2. Rabbit
3. Bird
4. Frog
5. Giraffe
6. Owl
7. Turtle
8. Duck
9. Eagle
10. Pig
11. Fish

## Ch. 3, page 54
## Match 'em Up

1. D,  2. C,
3. A,  4. B

## Ch. 4, page 73
## Find the Names

Sarah, Adam, Kim,
Carol, Tod, Mike,
Creg, Rachel, Ann,
Anna, Dan, Daniel,
Dave, Ashley, Tara,
Kris, Lea, Kala,
Jen, Ersa, Jan.

## Ch. 6, page 93
## Match 'em Up

1. Spoon, 2. Knife,
3. Glass, 4. Fork,
5. Plate, 6. Cup

## Ch. 7, page 109
## Find the Message

Sign Every Day

## Ch. 8, page 127
## What Are the Message?

1 Remind me.

2. That is mine.
3. I am hungry.
4. I need a haircut.
5. Do you like him?
6. Can you go?
7. What do you think?

## Ch. 9, page 137
## Which Number Is It?

A. 2
B. 4
C. 10
D. 1
E. 5
F. 3
G. 9
H. 7
J. 6
K. 8
L. 11

## Ch. 9, page 142
## Which Day Is It?

1. Wednesday
2. Friday
3. Saturday
4. Tuesday
5. Sunday
6. Monday
7. Thursday

## Ch. 10, page 167
## Are They Opposite?

1. No, (New/Knife)
2. Yes, (Same/Different)
3. Yes, (Hot/Cold)
4. Yes, (Expensive/Cheap)
5. No, (Come/Money)
6. Yes, (Start/Stop)

# Other Signing Books You Will Enjoy.